Jod Cassidy

"THIS BOOK SHOULD BE REQUIRED READING FOR EVERY PROSPECTIVE PUP PURCHASER TO CUT HIS CANINE TEETH ON."
—*The South Bend Tri*

In 16 years of practi_____ed more than 8,000_____d to perform trick_____sion, often right b_____s!

Because his enorm_____ful, easy-to-learn techniques are base____on a thorough understanding of canine psychology, he is able to explain not only what to do when training a dog, but also, what to do when efforts fail.

With actual, often hilarious case histories, he shows how owners can have dogs that are perfectly trained—and able to do obedience-trial stunts simply at a wave of the hand.

If you want to see how readily your dog can obey your commands,

buy and consult
PAUL LOEB'S COMPLETE BOOK OF DOG TRAINING

"Enhances the pleasure of owning a dog by helping the owner improve his relationship with his pet" —*The Baltimore News American*

PAUL LOEB'S COMPLETE BOOK OF DOG TRAINING

by PAUL LOEB

Drawings by Dale Payson

PUBLISHED BY POCKET BOOKS NEW YORK

POCKET BOOKS, a division of Simon & Schuster, Inc.
1230 Avenue of the Americas, New York, N.Y 10020

Copyright © 1974 by Paul Loeb

Front cover photo by Animals Animals/Paula Wright

Published by arrangement with Prentice-Hall, Inc.
Library of Congress Catalog Card Number: 74-9531

ISBN: 0-671-47297-6

First Pocket Books printing November, 1977

17 16 15 14 13 12 11 10 9 8

POCKET and colophon are registered trademarks
of Simon & Schuster, Inc.

Printed in the U.S.A.

To Stephanie

To our dogs:
Plum, Inches, Sleepy, and Snap
and to Tam, who put it all together

Foreword:

Who Is Paul Loeb?

Paul Loeb, a dog trainer for many years now, has written a most important contribution for people who own pets. He repeatedly demonstrates wisdom and insight into the often intimate relationships between owners and their dogs. By skillfully blending his own humorous experiences with his deep awareness of the psychological and emotional bonds between man and dog, Mr. Loeb teaches us all how to teach our dogs to be more enjoyable companions.

He draws on an extensive practice of training "companion animals" as well as more unusual and exotic creatures for movies and television. Step by step, the reader learns how to teach his or her dog the basic rules of obedience. And once learned, these rules become the basis for more complicated acts that a dog can then perform on command.

The need for patience and an awareness of an animal's special makeup are emphasized repeatedly throughout this clear, humane book. Both reader and pet are drawn closer together through understanding, and thereby, both their lives are enriched.

MARTIN DE ANGELIS, D.V.M.,
NEW YORK CITY

Contents

PART ONE
*What Dog Owners Should Know
But Usually Don't*   11

  1. My Philosophy on Dog Training   13
  2. The Love Fallacy   20
  3. Canine Development and Anatomy   29
  4. A Word on Clipping and Bathing   34
  5. Your Dog's Senses   37
  6. The Pack Theory   42
  7. Other Facets of Pack Behavior   49
  8. Between Human and Dog   54

PART TWO
Basic Care and Controlling Bad Habits   63

  9. Where Dog Owners Go Wrong   65
 10. Reprimands, the Word "No," and
     Body Language   71
 11. Feeding   76
 12. Chewing   83
 13. Paper Training and Basic Housebreaking   90
 14. Housebreaking the Older Dog   97
 15. What If He Breaks Training?   102
 16. Whining, Barking, and Jumping   107
 17. Biting   114
 18. Why Dogs Fight and Kill   118
 19. Adapting Your Dog to a Human
     Environment   121
 20. Traveling—Cars, Kennels, and Airplanes   126

PART THREE
Basic Obedience Training   135

21. Basic Training—for You   137
22. "Sit" and "Stay"   144
23. "Come"   152
24. "Lie Down"   157
25. "Heel"   162

PART FOUR
Tricks and Advanced Training   169

26. Tricks—an Introduction   171
27. "Roll Over" and "Play Dead"   176
28. Jumping—Over and Through   178
29. "Out" or "Go"   184
30. Carrying and Retrieving   187
31. Fetching by Scent Discrimination   191
32. Shopping   195
33. Diving and Surfing   199
34. Obedience Trials, Movies, and
    Commercials   205
35. Attack Dogs . . .   209
36. . . . Versus Defense Pets   215
37. Sniffing Out Bombs and Drugs   219

PART FIVE
From Birth to Death   225

38. Selecting Your Puppy   227
39. To Breed or Not to Breed?   235
40. Epilogue   240

    Index   243

Part One

WHAT
DOG OWNERS
SHOULD KNOW,
BUT
USUALLY
DON'T

1 My Philosophy on Dog Training

One Long Island socialite had a three-and-a-half year old Maltese, which she had trained herself. Assured that he was perfectly housebroken, she bought another to keep him company, and then had her entire house redecorated. The final result—with eighteenth-century antiques, oriental rugs, and fine engravings—was so splendid that soon she received a call from the feature editor of a top home-decoration magazine, who wanted to interview her and publish full-color pictures of her decorator's work.

The editor and photographer were shown in and settled themselves on a needlepoint couch. One of her Malteses sauntered into the room.

"Do your dogs ever mess up the house?" the editor asked, smiling.

"Never," the owner assured her. "I trained them both myself, and this one is perfectly housebroken."

With this, the "perfect" Maltese came closer, sniffed, and urinated copiously on the editor's shoe. The interview was quickly terminated.

The next morning the chagrined owner called me. Among other things, I explained that a "perfect" dog often regresses when a new dog enters the house. But there are techniques to stop this kind of behavior.

I have four dogs—three Malteses (Inches, Sleepy, and Snapper Dan) and a Weimaraner (Plum)—all of whom are totally housebroken. I will not have them lifting a leg in my apartment, which is full of large houseplants, and patchwork leather and suede couches and chairs fashioned entirely by hand by my wife Jo.

In addition to the dogs, I have a parrot, Martha (who won't talk but can bark), and a parakeet, Saturday. I also recently installed an eighty-gallon all-glass saltwater aquarium, with a number of damselfish, angelfish, and tangs. And last but not least, there's my daughter, Stephanie, who is the only one in the house who doesn't listen to me but whom I have to listen to when she practices on her piano or talks for hours on the phone to her friend Mary.

Plum, my Weimaraner, is a showpiece for my theories and techniques. He responds to voice, hand, and body commands with absolute precision. When I merely indicate an object with a gesture, he leaps over it with the grace of a gazelle. As a joke, he will steal a specific lady's purse on command. People are fascinated by his ability to bring back the magazines of my choice. I say, "Bring me *Time*." Plum passes by *Newsweek* and picks up *Time*.

I floored everyone in the bank one morning by asking the teller for one dollar bill and one one-hundred dollar bill, then having Plum successfully fetch me the larger denomination. However, my favorite feat is to send Plum out to shop for groceries. Given a basket and sent out the door, Plum makes his way to the proper shelves, tips cans of dog food into the basket, and trots up to the cashier, who, recognizing Plum, charges me for the day's basketful. Plum races home, careful not to spill, and gets a reward for his good work.

All the tricks in this book are ones that my dog has mastered. The training techniques I used to teach him are ones you will soon learn.

In some twelve years of working with animals, I have trained approximately eight thousand dogs for individual clients. In addition, I have trained the animal actors for hundreds of movies, TV commercials, and ads.

I grew up in Brooklyn, where I was first drafted into dog training when my father brought home a puppy named Tonto. He gave me and my two brothers four weeks to housebreak the dog.

The first three weeks we didn't bother to try to train him. Like all too many people, we thought that training takes care of itself. As the four week deadline approached, Tonto was still untrained. The three of us, fearful of having to give the puppy away, set up round-the-clock watches of eight hours each. Tonto would misbehave, be punished, be taken out again and again—and finally shaped up.

The next dog I got was after I had left home. I started training him, and almost immediately I noticed a great difference between him and the dogs we had as children. I realized that it's the *owner* who makes a dog what he is. I soon became so fascinated by this principle that I began devoting all my free time to training the dog and researching the effect that people have on their dogs. I never thought of making a business out of training dogs, I was just fascinated by the whole relationship between dogs and people and wanted to find out as much as I could about the subject.

I read as many books as possible, researched every conceivable training method, including military training, police training, hunting, obedience, trick, and anything else you can think of. I spoke and worked with many different trainers. Some I learned from, others learned from me. But this just wasn't enough. *Nobody* could explain the one thing I wanted to know more than anything else—the human element. Nobody's dog is the same as anybody else's. No dog responds in quite the same way as another. Therefore, I started to research dog *owners* and not just dogs, and in order to do this I had to start working with them.

By this point, I had made a fair amount of money in the Seventh Avenue garment industry—a job I really didn't care for. I left and devoted my time to researching owner/dog dynamics.

That was the beginning of my career. Since then, I have made many personal TV and radio appearances across the country and abroad. Whenever I'm on, the questions run pretty much the same from program to program:

"How do you stop a dog from chewing?"

"My dog bit someone. He used to be so gentle. Why did he do that?"

"How do you stop a dog from pulling you down the street?"

"How do you stop a dog from relieving himself in the house?"

"What kind of dog will go with ours?"

"We would like to mate our dog. Can you set it up?"

"Did you train the dog in this commercial? Or that movie?"

(When the inevitable leopard-coat question comes up, I simply reiterate that it should be left on the leopard. The only skins we should use are those of animals raised for food.)

At home, the questions continue. My desk is an architect's drawing board, and calls come in constantly to either of two phones on the floor of my cluttered foyer. Callers often want a little something extra for their dime, especially free advice. They call up and say things like "What kind of progress are you making in the study of animal behavior?" Or "What is your method of making a saluki sit?"*

Very few diagnoses can be made over the phone, and I am most adamant about working with the owner and dog in their own environment, the home. Some dogs have more problems than others—or, rather, some *people* have more problems than others. And, of course, certain cases deserve special attention.

I don't always succeed in my goals, however. A convent of nuns on the West Side tried to engage me, but when they found out that I had to come to their residence, they changed their minds. No man had ever been inside the convent, and they would not budge from their firm policy.

But the client's home is where the dog's habit patterns are formed and where all the training should be solved. That's where the rug is being soiled, where the curtains are being chewed, so that's where we work the problem out. If the dog has trouble behaving in supermarkets, I work with him in supermarkets.

In one secretary's apartment, the furniture was all scarred because "Baby" had been chewing everything in sight, and his mistress didn't know how to stop him. He was her first dog, and like most people, she didn't know how to handle him.

The dog was six months old, and I would rather he were six weeks. By six months, a puppy has had time to pick up bad habits that have to be removed. At six weeks, he hasn't had as much opportunity to make mistakes, and if properly trained, he can be more easily molded to his owner's way of life.

With this particular dog, the first thing I did was to discard the greasy steak bone he had been chewing. I ex-

---

* Salukis are fascinating dogs. They move very deliberately, much like an antelope, and are very alert. They are the oldest hunting dogs on record, and are pictured in ancient Egyptian tomb paintings.

plained to the owner that every spot that a greasy bone touches will absorb grease and meat odors—and thereby becomes a potentially nice place for chewing.

When I entered the apartment of my next client the cocker spaniel immediately jumped up on me, and I carefully flipped him over backward, saying "no"—one way to stop a dog from jumping up on people. The cocker quickly retreated to his special closet—from which he attacked anyone who went near him.

As a puppy, he had been sent there as a punishment after being reprimanded. He soon learned that he could avoid a reprimand by running to his closet whenever he felt he might be punished. Surrounded by walls on three sides, where a human could get at him only by bending down and reaching in, he felt very secure. He knew he had the advantage there, and he took it.

This spaniel had a lot of other problems too—urinating on the rug, shoe chewing, nipping the children. As is customary, I wanted to see how the family acted with this dog. I had to meet every member of the household to assess the difficulties involved. I wanted to find out what was the cause of this behavior problem, and so I tried to get a complete history of the dog.

In this particular case, it was very obvious that the owners were at fault. I explained that what they thought was punishment—putting him in the closet—was in fact a lesson in aggression for the dog. By putting him in the closet, they had unknowingly given him a "fortress" from which he could strike, a way for him to control *them*. And when he saw what he could get away with, he, like any other animal, decided to take advantage of the situation.

What had to be done with this dog was to take away his security spot, neutralize his aggression, and teach him some good habits. And it had to be done in this order, or it wouldn't have worked.

At another stop, a more technological—and expensive —approach was needed to control an obstreperous pet. The dog was left to wander alone through the apartment, while I watched his actions on the screen of a closed-circuit TV monitor outside. Whenever the dog started to chew furniture, urinate, or literally tear up the house, I would say "no" into an intercom mike, and my voice was amplified many times by a speaker inside the apartment.

The animal quickly shaped up. This is a rather expensive way to train dogs, but sometimes, as in this case, there is no alternative.

By this time, of course, you've realized that it's the owners who are my pupils. And if I feel a person won't follow my advice, I won't take him as a client. There's little point in taking a dog and training him to *my* way of life. The dog is living with his owner, not with me, and he should be trained by him and not me. I theorize that, since most problems come from the owner and not the dog, the owner should be taught to understand the dog and his role in the dog's life, and vice versa.

Now and again I have had to retrain dogs who have been to other training schools. Some of these trainers never *fully* explain the dynamics of dog behavior and owner-and-dog relationship. They simply lay down a series of iron-clad rules and employ inexperienced help who train strictly according to the rule book, with little or no flexibility.

The owner is seldom if ever warned to expect occasional breakdowns in discipline or given instructions on what to do if the dog errs. After the usual contractual time limit of six to eight weeks is over, the owner's complaints are answered in one of two standard ways: "Your dog is untrainable." Or "It's your fault."

In general, I visit my clients once a week, and if there is a problem with their dog, I ask them to call between visits. When there are absolutely no calls from a new client, I *know* there's a giant list of problems. Nobody can have a perfect dog in the first two weeks. Dogs are living things and, like us, are all subject to idiosyncrasies.

I consider my work a practice, not a business. I have no set rules for training. Each dog is a new experience, just as each family is unique—and therefore the problems and causes of these problems are different. When I listen to people talking about their dogs, I usually find they don't know too much about dog behavior. So training must start at the most basic point, the beginning.

The first thing I do is to try to make my clients feel relaxed. I want people to think of training their dogs as enjoyable rather than a chore. The most important principle in my training technique, however, is transference—making sure the dog recognizes his owner, not me, as the authority figure. I try to take advantage of a dog's natural pack instincts, only substituting the dog's owner as the dominant pack leader. The dog should never be a leader but always a member.

When people ask me to spell out dog-training techniques and care, I find that stories about other owners and their dogs is the best way of illustrating dog problems and their solutions. This book, then, is full of my experiences and case histories, and shows what happens if exercises are *not* done correctly. You can learn from your own as well as others' mistakes.

This book should entertain you as well as instruct you, and the lessons apply to owners of mixed-breed dogs as well as to owners of purebreds. Your dog can probably learn as many as eighty or even a hundred commands in his lifetime, and by following my instructions in this book, you can teach him to do almost anything within reason. It's a good idea to read this book completely through, however, before starting any training at all. Once your dog's entire makeup is clear to you, you'll find it easier to do the right thing automatically. And knowing the full range of feats that dogs *can* perform will give you greater confidence for the more elementary steps.

2 The Love
Fallacy

One of the chief reasons we have difficulty understanding dogs is, paradoxically, because they've been associated with us for such a long time—so much so that we take them for granted.

The first evidence of dog's association with man is found at the Mesolithic site of Star Carr in England about 9500 B.C., when the dog's superior sense of smell probably directed man to within bowshot of food animals.

Recently in the ruins of Pompeii the lava casts of the bodies of a little boy and his huge dog were found. On the dog's bronze collar was the still legible inscription: "This dog has saved his little master three times—once from fire, once from drowning, and once from thieves." The dog had obviously tried to rescue his master once more.*

In England, medals and trophies are awarded for canine bravery. One is the National Canine Defence League Medal, the dog's version of the Victoria Cross. Swansea Jack, a black retriever, saved twenty-seven people from drowning at the Swansea Docks and was awarded the dog's V.C. Chum was decorated by the Duke of Gloucester for bravery in saving two people from a fire. The dog was sixteen years old.

John Garfield once turned down a film role which re-

* Very few domestic animals were found in the archaeological excavations of Pompeii. Animals instinctively know of impending catastrophe, and obviously most of the dogs fled before the eruption occurred. The night before the San Francisco earthquake in 1906, dogs barked strangely. Horses snorted and stampeded minutes before anyone realized what was going on. In the mountains of Sicily, people leave their houses should the dogs suddenly exit.

quired him to mistreat a dog. "Slapping women, robbing kids, yes, but the public would never forgive anyone who kicked a dog."

One of my most unforgettable clients was a man in his forties who had built a towering reputation in New York's manufacturing community. Midway through his executive life, he acquired a Newfoundland puppy. He found that he had barely enough time to play with the dog when he came home in the evening. Most owners would compromise with such a full schedule, but not this gentleman. He retired from his enormously successful business and moved away from his family. During the winters he and the Newfoundland went to live in Florida, where he served as a cabana attendant. In the summers he came north again, to tend bar and have the full day to spend with his dog.

For seven years he relished his full-time companionship, never missing his previously wealthy life. Then tragedy struck; the Newfoundland became ill with a spine problem. Over $10,000 was spent on surgery and recuperation kennels, but the dog was still unable to walk. His owner hired physiotherapists to take the dog swimming each day in the surf—but to no avail, and eventually he had his pet put to sleep.

Heartbroken, the man no longer had any excuse to keep on with his nomadic existence. He went back to his old line of work, and in a few short months, he had turned a few inventive ideas into a fortune. This brought him no particular joy, but his success was a thorn in the side of his competitors who retaliated—if you can call it that—by leaving another lovely puppy literally on the doorstep of his brownstone. And indeed, he became so involved with his new pet that again he left his business to spend his waking hours with a four-legged companion.

An unhappy majority of the population work at jobs they don't like, taking orders from others, forced to hold back their emotions. When they return home in the evening, their only emotional outlet is through their family or their pets. Those who live alone have no immediate family, so they use the dog to balance the day's ledgers—either by being nice or being nasty. When they realize that the animal will accept them with no backtalk, they usually look forward to coming home and enjoying their animal. I always remind owners that the ultimate one-to-one relationship is with another *person*. But if a man wants to take a walk after supper to relax and do some heavy thinking, who does he choose to take along—his wife, his kids, or the dog?

People can tell a dog anything, be inconsistent and ill-tempered, and still be assured of faithful love. Some people tell me that if it weren't for their dogs, they couldn't have gotten through moments of stress. When I'm bothered about certain things, I find it relaxing just walking and playing and even talking to my dog. My wife finds pleasure holding her dog in her arms and dancing with him to some good music. I hate to admit it, but if I had to choose between saving my dog and a total human stranger I would probably save the dog.

Check the daily listings in the newspapers lost-and-found column to see how much the average dog can mean to its owners.

And once a dog is adopted into the family, no expense seems too high to be justified. An interesting example of this occurred to a New York couple, each of whom was extremely wrapped up in a career. They acquired a collie and since neither was able to walk the animal on any regular schedule, a professional dog walking service was hired. When the husband complained about the bills, the wife told him simply, "It's too late. The dog is already part of the family."

The status conscious will pick a breed that's very showy and obviously very expensive: a saluki, Afghan, or Russian wolfhound. The dogs that New York's swinging singles pick are all very good measurements of what the owners want you to think of them. But the owners who worry me are those who choose certain breeds to compensate for their own deficiencies.

Some people want very aggressive dogs because either they are, or want to be, aggressive people. Specifically, I find that many owners themselves are physically shy and feel put-upon. So they choose a dog who's anything but. The most common problem, of course, is that the shy master finds it difficult to control an animal he has already decided is "stronger" than he is.

Many people consider their dog a human being, or at least a creature who appreciates the same luxuries we do. Who hasn't seen households with covered-up chairs for the dog's comfort, televisions turned to a certain channel "for the dogs"?

On Park Avenue, there's a poodle who lives in the utmost of style. He has steps up to his bed so that he doesn't have to jump. A rubber mat lies under his sheets, which are changed daily by a maid hired especially for this purpose. The poodle is fed pâté, caviar, and champagne, and has a tailor-made wardrobe. His mistress doesn't want to inhibit him in any way.

A middle-aged woman called me to check on what supplies she would need for a weekend trip to the Poconos. When questioned what she had already added to the carload, she listed dog deodorizer, foam cushions, food, water bowls, chew bones, toys, a spatula, and a *New York Times*. My question was where was she going to rest up the next weekend after unloading the car. (When I went on a 13,000-mile camping trip, I took four dogs, one wife, two sleeping bags, and one tent.)

Thumb through your weekly magazines and see exactly how people are expected to say "I love you" to their dogs. A sample list:

Vuitton's 14-inch pet tote	$150.00
Madeira wicker carrying basket	14.50
Breath Sweet hard rubber ball	3.00
Breath Sweet hard rubber pull ring	3.00
Grooming rake	1.65
Oval scrub brush	2.80
Wicker igloo w/red plaid cushion	18.00
Stainless steel trimming shears	15.50
Rolled natural leather leash	9.00
Plaid wool coat	10.00
Non-tarnish all aluminum food/water dish	5.00
Ceramic bowl	3.00
Oster stainless steel airjet hair dryer	36.00
Wooden handled wire grooming brush	2.80
Wire "slicker" brush	2.50
Metal comb	2.50
Rubber shampoo brush	1.90
Grooming mitt	5.00
Gold-plated chain leads	7.00
Brass collar bell from India	1.00
Braided leather lead	5.00

For people who get really involved with dogs as family, there's *Our Puppy's Baby Book*. The book includes sec-

tions for all those things you'd want to remember about
your child: early snapshots, birth date, first paw print,
feeding charts, health records, handling instructions, family trees (actual or imaginary), famous firsts like barks,
fights, trips, dog shows, ribbons, and so forth. There's even
a section for people he has met, i.e., mailman, paper boy,
milkman, grocer.

These canine indulgences obviously give the owner more
pleasure than the dog, and what's wrong with that? When
a person starts treating a dog like a human being, however, he often begins *thinking* of him as one. And this is
where the owner/pet relationship begins to break down.

I asked one new client for a list of the things he felt
were wrong with his dog. Naturally I expected a string of
bad habits, such as not sitting on command or chewing
the rug, but the man took me too seriously and submitted
a list of human problems. He asserted he could tell that
the dog was emotionally disturbed by the way he ate his
food, by the way he walked down the street and played,
and especially by the way his stool came out. The man
said that his dog had no ambition, no motivation, was
emotionally unhappy, didn't work well in groups and
had severe jealousy hang-ups.

Many owners say that their dog reacts a certain way
because of some human trait that they are used to dealing
with. An enthusiastic hairdresser was explaining his difficulty in housebreaking his Doberman: "He's exactly
like I am. Stubborn, uncontrollable, and totally erratic."
One psychologist asserted that his dog "only responds in
group therapy." In reality the dog stopped chewing up
his master's shoes simply because of all the new attention
that the "encounter group" lavished on him. Once the
group began meeting elsewhere, the dog was thrown on
his own again and resumed chewing out of boredom.

One client had trouble reconciling the fact that his poodle wouldn't come to him. He felt the poodle was rejecting
him and demonstrating it in this way. The dog was trained
to come long before his master got over his rejection complex.

One woman was actively involved in weekly visits to her
psychiatrist who was convinced that radical confrontation
was the way to mental health. He told her to scream out
whatever her problems were. The poor dog who had to
listen to all of this *Sturm and Drang* was a wreck. I ad-

vised her to scream at her husband if she felt the need, but not at her dog.

Then there's the lady who thought her dog was suicidal. Every day the dog went out on a glass-doored patio, looked around, and came back in. Finally, the dog broke through the glass door, wound up with severe cuts, and he was immediately taken to a veterinarian. His owner now told the vet that the dog was in shock. His cuts were not bleeding much, and when people are in shock, they don't bleed. The veterinarian thanked her for her diagnosis and asked her please to wait outside.

The dog was in no way suicidal, I pointed out, but a victim of circumstance. He was locked up every day, and was taken out only once. He simply wanted out. He went to the glass door, not expecting to find it shut. The family was particularly neat and had cleaned the glass hours before.

Human beings walk through plate-glass doors all the time. This dog simply did the same. I told the owner in no uncertain terms that her dog's life was in her hands. It was up to her to see that he was walked at least four times per day, and to make sure that safety bars were put on the doors.

Yet another lady wanted to know if there was a dog IQ test. I informed her that a dog's intelligence has nothing to do with how well he's trained. If the feat required of him is reasonable, he can probably accomplish it. Don't ask him to push the elevator buttons, because he's not manually dextrous, but to come when called is not too much to ask!

I often hear statements such as "I tell my dog he's doing something wrong, and he goes right on doing it. But then, he's a Leo, and must have his own way." Whenever I hear something to this effect, I feel sure that the dog is spoiled rotten. It's sometimes easier to relate to a client through his or her fantasies.

Giving human characteristics to dogs is not advisable, and even though at times he almost appears human, a dog is not programmed to respond to human psychology.

In the wild a strong male can have his pick of females. In your home his sex life has to be curtailed and controlled. In the wild he can lift his leg and move his bowels as many times and in as many places as he wants. In your home there are schedules and specific places where he must go. In the wild he can run free. In your home he must learn to walk on a leash. In the wild he can bark and howl at the moon. But you have to think of the neighbors.

A small proportion of dog owners go through life not training their dogs in simple canine terms. As a result, they put up with a lot of nonsense. One psychologist let his great Dane take over the whole apartment. I walked in to see all the chairs covered, rugs kicked back, and clothing strewn all over the room. "Well," says the embarrassed dog owner, "he likes it that way."

"But," I asked, "do *you* like it that way?"

"I get used to it."

One dog chewed up a complete room, so the owner gave him the room, saying, "It's his. He likes it. He can have it."

I am seldom surprised by the many ways in which a dog can adapt to man. What does startle me is the ways in which owners adapt to their dogs. One family felt that they couldn't possibly train their dog not to chew or urinate in the house. So they had their living room installed with a lovely wrought-iron gate to protect the corner with their choice belongings. In cases like this it's hard to determine whether it's the owner or the dog who's being confined for bad behavior.

Untrained dogs should have certain areas where they do belong, as well as off-limit regions. One particularly congenial Manhattan woman with just such a dog called me a meanie for wanting to place restrictions on him. She felt her dog should be allowed complete run of the house. But a week after her new shag rug arrived, she had boards installed across the living-room doorway.

One doctor encourages his spaniel to jump up and nuzzle his hand. Without knowing it he could be training the dog to bite. The dog has taken to knocking mailmen and milkmen down the front steps, and the doctor's wife says that "If he weren't so pretty, I'd get rid of him." This family has no real concept of what's happening to their dog. In any case, it's pretty hard to perform surgery with only one hand.

There's a lady whose Afghan refuses to come when she calls him. So whenever she takes him out to the park for a run, she comes prepared to wait for him usually all day! She can't make any other appointments. "He usually comes back around four o'clock," she guarantees.

One particular owner claimed his dog was really well-trained. For some reason, he never seemed to notice him barking, biting, chasing other dogs and children, and being a general nuisance.

Another client informed me that his German shepherd was thoroughly housebroken. "He only messes in the house once a day, only chews things I don't need anymore." Other than that, he'll be the first to admit, the dog is perfect.

A woman once called me in for a visit, complaining that her animal was a barker, a biter, and generally obnoxious. But her husband felt he was in complete control of the dog: "I have no problem with him." To demonstrate, the man opened his car door and the dog obediently jumped into the back seat on command. However, as the owner settled himself in the driver's seat, the dog began barking furiously. The owner turned in his seat and said, "Now be quiet," in a firm voice. His dog bit him on the nose.

Every family claims to love its dog. But what is love? What seems right to you isn't necessarily right for your dog. Many people proclaim that they give their dog total freedom out of love, but what about discipline? That is part of love too. He needs the discipline of someone saying no, as well as praise and rewards when he does things properly.

Certain individuals say, "You'll break the dog's spirit." Some are afraid that disciplining the dog will make the animal feel unloved. This is the exact same reason they refuse to discipline their children, and often have the same kind of obedience dilemmas with them. In one case the daughter of a client told me that her family had once had another dog that they couldn't housebreak. "Mommy was afraid he would wet on the rugs, so she made us keep him in the bathroom all the time."

Dogs and children both want and need to be disciplined. They crave the security this kind of authority affords them. As long as reprimands are not overly harsh and don't become a way of life and are balanced with a lot of affection and tender loving care, your dog should develop into a well-trained *and* happy pet.

Some owners find their dogs are just too much trouble. They lose their patience in training and give up. I get lots of calls from people who thought (and rightly so) dogs were for fun, but somehow just can't cope with the details of ownership. "Do you want to buy a dog?" they inquire politely. "He's four years old, and we want him to have a special, healthy home."

I ask them why they want to get rid of the dog. Among the many answers I get, the most common is "We're moving." To where? "None of your business." There's no whimper of care in the conversation, just a pretense of finding a "nice home." Someone wants to get rid of a potentially marvelous pet that just hasn't been trained properly.

There are many strays wandering the streets day and night, looking for food and shelter. Where do they come from? All too often they are the unwanted victims of "love" substituted for discipline. That "nice home in the country" often turns out to be some deserted area where the owner can dump his pet to forage and fend for himself, without too many witnesses to make him feel guilty.

You can see your dog running in his dreams. It's almost as though he smiles or chases a rabbit, or is in pain. It's safe to bet he dreams just as we do. But remember *your dog is not a person*. Never confuse his life with yours. You are a breed apart, and you must accept him *as a dog* and train him as such. This brief fact is the key to years of rewarding relationship with your pet. And to train him properly, it's absolutely vital to understand his basic makeup—how he thinks, what his body demands of him, what he responds to, and what instincts have made him the way he is.

3 Canine Development and Anatomy

Where did dogs evolve from? We don't know. Many theories, including the one that a dog was once a domesticated jackal, have been discredited. In the years I have been investigating this question, I have yet to come up with a satisfactory answer. It is known, however, that dogs did not evolve from wolves, but rather both evolved from some common ancestor. To put it another way, a wolf is to a dog what a chimpanzee is to man. The latter did not "descend" from the former. Each pair represents the end products of parallel evolution. But all breeds of dogs do belong to the same species, as was recently proved when a dachshund bitch gave birth to a healthy litter sired by a St. Bernard!

When a dog gives birth to a litter of puppies, she does all the training, instilling them with the basic techniques of survival, until they're about six weeks old. Then it's time for you to take over. Naturally, if a puppy has been taken from his mother before that time, it's up to you to be both mother and trainer.

If the newly separated puppy cries, the old trick of placing a ticking clock and hot-water bottle nearby will probably calm him down. But not because he associates the ticking with her heartbeat and the heat with her body warmth. A dog's body temperature naturally falls during sleep (as does ours or any warm-blooded animal's), and a small puppy's body volume is often too small to retain much heat and keep him from getting chilled. You'll see that puppies in a pet shop window usually take naps under, around, or atop other sleeping puppies all piled together like a bin of discount goods. Being next to another warm body simply helps the sleeping dog regulate the fluctuations in his body temperature. Therefore, the hot-water bottle makes your puppy more comfortable.

As for the ticking clock, it simply provides a regular, constant, familiar, and comforting sound, and helps to mask other small noises that might unnerve him if they were heard in an utterly quiet room. A puppy is used to constant fuss and racket from his brothers and sisters, and the sudden silence and solitude of his new home affects him much as a first night in the country affects a lifelong city dweller, who becomes grateful for the chirp of crickets.

In estimating a dog's lifetime, most people count seven "people" years for each year of a dog's life. But I feel that the first year of a dog's life is the equal of fifteen human years. At the age of one, your dog is an adolescent, still learning his limitations and not yet physically mature. This accelerated development emphatically points out the difference between a dog and a child. At three months, a dog can understand much more than a baby of the same age. At sixteen weeks a dog is able to sit, stay, lie down, and heel on command. No human baby can possibly master so many responses so quickly.

By age two, he's added nine more "human" years. He's now sexually mature, and grows only in strength and general *savoir-faire*. After the age of two, he ages at the rate of five "human years" a year. The years from two to five see a male dog grow from a young stripling to a mature, dominant animal. He's smarter now, mentally and physically, and by age five, he's reached his peak, in full control of himself and his environment. This is prime time for the male dog. By this time the owner should know him pretty well and have figured out his quirks and idiosyncrasies, and the dog has learned to accept what the master lays down—or vice versa. The dog retains his peak until about age seven (forty-nine "human years"). And then, though his physical strength tapers off, his mental capabilities do not, and he becomes "a smart old fox." By this modified time table, a fifteen-year-old dog (not an uncommon age) is not a canine Methuselah, but about eighty-nine in human terms, which is not an uncommon age for anyone to reach.

Owners question me about the normalcy of their dogs.

What is normalcy? Years of study make the answer available. Each dog is unique, of course, but certain patterns repeat constantly, making problem solving less of a labyrinth than it could be. Circling, for example, is usually normal. Dogs walk in circles for various reasons. It is instinctive before defecation and before bedding down, since in the wild, it's far more comfortable to beat down the prickly grass before lying or squatting. Dogs also circle when about to fight or play—just to get into an advantageous position or to expend nervous tension.

Show me a dog who's in a bad way, and I can usually show you a master who's not observant, who can't see the obvious.

A great majority of people feel a dog is helpless since he can't talk. When your dog is in pain, he can most certainly tell you. Dogs have a way of moping around, coming up to you and nudging you. Although they can't tell you where it hurts, their behavior patterns do alter.

An abnormal dog is simply one who acts odd to the practiced eye. I don't claim to be qualified in medicine, all I am is an animal trainer. However, I do refer people to veterinarians who are able to tell if the dog is physically healthy.

Dogs are living creatures and should be treated with concern. One client called to say his dog had been hit by a car. I told him that he ought to see a veterinarian who, in this client's case, lived just down the block. Half an hour later, I dropped by to check, and found the owner still puttering around while his dog—whose leg appeared to be broken—was apparently suffering acute pain.

Common sense is good for about 75 percent of all dog problems, but for the remaining 25 percent, you have to know a little about biology, chemistry, and sometimes plain natural history. For example, one worried owner complained about a rapidly growing tumor in his dog's ear. I checked it out and found that the "tumor" was in reality a blood-gorged tick, which I quickly pulled off. The bump's gray color matched that of the dog's skin, and the owner panicked. What had happened was that the animal had recently romped through some long, country grass and picked up some ticks. (By the way, never apply a lighted cigarette to dislodge a tick. It's too easy to injure your dog.)

A normal dog's anatomy has a few features that may

seem decidedly *ab*normal to the novice owner. For one
thing, most owners soon notice that a dog's skin fits him
very loosely. A basset hound's soulful gaze is partly the
result of his facial skin being too large for the skull—
hence the drooping eyelids. This is primarily a defensive
adaptation. Unless another dog can get a grip on the
underlying muscle, the bitten dog can still maneuver within
his skin for a better position. For the same reason, a dog's
skin is provided only lightly with blood vessels. When a
dog's skin is laid open, he will bleed only slightly unless,
of course, the underlying tissue is damaged. Similarly,
his skin is provided with only a sprinkling of pain recep-
tors.

Many people are surprised to learn that our sense of
touch comprises at least five subsenses: sensitivity to pressure, temperature (heat and cold), and pain, among
others. A dog's skin is relatively insensitive to pain. To
get an idea of what it feels like to be inside your dog's
skin, pinch the fold of wrinkled skin right over your elbow
as hard as you can. This pinch, which would bring sharp
pain to other parts of your body, produces only a mildly
uncomfortable sensation. Your elbow takes a great deal of
abrasions and abuse, and there's no point in having
your "alarm system" constantly jangling. However, the
muscles and bones immediately beneath your elbow are
exquisitely sensitive, as you learn whenever you jolt your
funny bone. This is your body's way of saying that an
injury to the skin in this area is standard wear and tear,
but an injury that reaches any deeper is worth knowing
about.

So it is with your dog's skin. If you decide to punish him
by hitting his flank with a magazine, the blow may be
about as troubling as a pinch on your elbow.

Your dog has a higher tolerance to pain and a lower
awareness of it than you do. For example, a man with a
bad leg will still favor it when he crosses the street to
meet a beautiful girl he hasn't seen in months. A dog with
an injured leg will race right across to get to a bitch in
heat. The dog's desire is simply stronger than his aversion
to pain, and so he puts it aside.

You must remember that pain is not a deterrent in itself,
not even to human beings. One anthropologist passed out
a number of safety pins to members of an aboriginal tribe
who'd never seen such things before. A short time later he
returned to find the native children gleefully inserting the

pins through their lower lips! The pins couldn't have been comfortable, but the novelty and excitement of discovery were more compelling than physical distress.

All dogs have a layer of fat beneath the skin that provides all the insulation they need for cold weather. And some dogs have a double coat consisting of long silky hairs and a woolly undercoat. A dog's skin has another unique feature, a total absence of sweat glands. This is an evolutionary adaptation to aid the dog in hunting game. With no sweat glands, the dog's body odor is far less distinct, so that other animals will have trouble locating the dog by scent alone. Even a filthy dog smells "cleaner" than a well-groomed horse, for instance.

But now that a dog no longer hunts for a living, his lack of sweat glands are less of an advantage. Heat will bother him much more than it would you. Dogs have a natural instinct to dig, to hide something, to find something, or just for the pleasure of digging. On a very hot day, a dog will often dig holes in the ground under bushes to find a damp layer of the earth, protected from the sun's rays, to lie in and thereby cool himself off.

Many pets die each summer from being left in parked cars. If he has no way to cool himself except by panting, a dog's body will soon heat up. If he goes to sleep, his metabolism—and hence his internal body temperature—will be lowered. But if sleep is impossible or ineffective, he may go into shock—a natural response to put the brakes on metabolism, but one that can be fatal to the dog.

4 A Word on Clipping and Bathing

Some long-haired dogs do not need their hair as much to keep them warm as to screen them from the heat of the sun. The Mexican hairless has a tough, crusty skin to deflect the sun's rays. A Maltese or Yorkie has a silky outer coat, but no woolly undercoat, so if either of these dogs is shaved close, the sun can blister the skin, and the dog can get sunstroke more quickly. Therefore, the misguided owner who clips his pet every summer "to help the poor thing stay cool" is sabotaging the dog's own air-conditioning system at the very time he needs it most! However, if you keep your dog indoors most of the time, it shouldn't make much difference. Most dogs shed their hair constantly all year round, with exceptionally heavy shedding occurring about twice a year. (This is why I recommend a weekly brushing to remove loose hair and avoid its winding up on rugs and furniture.) But no dog, not even a poodle, ever requires clipping except for cosmetic reasons.

The poodle's distinctive cut, incidentally, evolved from the breed's original use as a hunting dog. Left to its own devices, a poodle will develop a curly bathmat "afro" which gives it the approximate appearance of an English sheepdog. But this curly hair tended to pick up weeds and refuse whenever a poodle entered the water, and so most of the body hair was clipped to increase the animal's aquatic efficiency.

Skin odor may be a warning sign that your dog has contracted seborrhea, a common disorder among pets. There are two distinct types—one where your dog has oily skin, and one where he has very dry skin that flakes off like dandruff. A very unpleasant odor accompanies either of these symptoms. Your veterinarian will instruct you in what medication to use. Forget perfume—it only adds to the problem.

Many owners spray their dogs with artificial scents to camouflage the fact that the animal needs a bath, but the truth of the matter is that sweet-smelling perfumes contain alcohol, which could dry out your dog's skin. Use perfume only on a ribbon or some item that he wears.

Wash your dog at reasonable intervals. Once every three to four months is enough. But brush him regularly—every day if he's a long-haired breed. You should have solid determination when you wash your dog. A sodden dog often makes such a flood that the owner shies away from ever trying it again.

A sink or bathtub will do for bathing your dog and there's only a few simple rules to follow:

1. *Get him used to the bathroom and tub. This makes the later bathing easier. Don't turn on any water, just bring him into the bathroom and praise him. Place a towel or something in the tub so that your dog can get a secure footing, because if he slips or does not feel secure, he will jump out, and you will have a very tough time getting him back in. Then put him in the tub and praise him again. Give him a treat such as a cookie—show him it's fun to be there. Increase the time he has to stay in the tub. Make the time sufficient for you to give him a good bath.*

2. *Long-haired dogs should be brushed out thoroughly before bathing or their hair will become matted and tangled. Use a mild soap or baby shampoo. Don't dunk him in any soaps with chemical additives, even if the labels say they're harmless.*

3. *Keep the door closed when bathing him because he might decide to leave the bathroom in the middle of his bath. If he gets out, he can do a lot of staining and tracking, and a soapy dog is as hard to handle as a greased pig.*

4. *Drain all the water out of the tub before you take your pet out, but be sure to keep him away from the drain, because the suction might frighten him. When the water is drained, he will then shake him-*

self off a few times, and the mess will be kept at a minimum. Dry him—and yourself—off as best you can.

I wash Plum when the spirit moves me. On warm mornings I send him swimming after a stick I throw in a pond, lake, or river. By the time he retrieves it, he's thoroughly wet. I then soap him down with baby soap and throw the stick out in the pond again—Plum retrieves it and at the same time rinses himself off.

5 Your Dog's Senses

In training your dog, you must know exactly what it is that he responds to.

Everyone has heard of the Russian scientist Ivan Pavlov who conditioned his dogs to salivate at the sound of a bell. But don't confuse this with training. His laboratory dogs would *automatically* salivate when the bell rang because their brain cells had associated the sound with food. They were not *obeying* Pavlov, but were simply prisoners of their own nervous systems' association patterns.

By contrast, most of what I teach dogs—and what you will want to teach your own pet—are not simple knee-jerk responses, but *conscious* behavior on the part of the animal. A well-trained dog is not a robot. He is perfectly able to disobey you, but doesn't because his desire for approval and praise from his master—and his respect for his master's dominance—override whatever satisfaction he gets from doing his own thing.

Another trainer once asked me if a dog could be trained to cross the street only when the "walk" light was on. I explained that he couldn't, simply because he has trouble differentiating between certain colors at a distance. Some breeds do not have good eyesight to begin with. The "sight" hunting dogs (Afghan, saluki, greyhound, wolf-hound, etc.) have the very best eyesight, but even they find it easier to recognize moving targets than stationary shapes. Plum can recognize the difference between *Time* and *Newsweek*, but only at close range. The stop-and-go signals a dog could respond to best, would have to be directed to his keener sense of smell and hearing. A whistle for stop and silence for go, or vice versa, would work, but a giant atomizer alternately spraying aromas of meat and vinegar seems one device that will never be patented. A pity, because it would certainly appeal to a dog's best-developed sense.

One dog owner was amazed that her beagle could smell her coming home, even after she had rinsed herself thoroughly at the beach. But this is simply because a dog's sense of smell is at least seven times as acute as ours, and a beagle is one of the tops in olfactory acuity. It makes sense when you realize that your dog's ancestors used to hunt for a living. A dog's nose is particularly attuned to acids—so acutely that he can distinguish one part acid dissolved in a solution of 1 million parts water! Your sweat contains nitrogenous wastes which have an acid content, and since the most cleansing shower still leaves some minute traces of sweat on the skin, a dog can smell it out.

Psychologists are just recognizing that all animals crave stimulus, call it variety, almost as much as they do food and sex. A dog loves to go out because he *needs* all of the stimuli, such as new smells, he picks up outside. His sense of smell is his most highly developed sense, so it is through smell that he gets most of his information about the world around him.

Even a dog's call to the opposite sex is controlled by an odor. (Humans use the same principle on a much subtler, sophisticated, and controlled level. What do you think perfume is for?) Your dog's sense of smell explains a great deal of his behavior.

Cat droppings and horse manure are great delicacies for dogs—they eat them with gusto. Dog-food companies know all about a dog's love for a strong odor. Haven't you noticed that most dog foods have a very strong smell? The stronger the smell, the more a dog loves it, so if your pet isn't eating too well, try putting some very strong cheese in his food.

You know how your dog loves to lick your face in the early morning. Well, it's not only out of attachment, it's also because dogs love bad breath. Owners always figure that the dog drags their underwear around out of affection. It's actually the odor that intrigues him. If your pet seems overly affectionate, check all the local smells.

When you take your dog to the beach or to the park, you may see him rolling on the ground as if he were scratching his back. The reason he does this is because there is, or was, the carcass of a dead animal or the wastes of an animal of a species *other than a dog* on that spot.

This is a natural instinctive action, a form of odor camouflage. The nondog aroma effectively covers his natural odors and in this way throws off any possible predator, who will not be interested in the smell of feces or carrion. (It goes without saying that neither will you!) Also, rolling in the odor of a carcass or the carcass itself is an aggressive action, a dog's sign of victory—a *coup de grâce*.

What's behind the anus-sniffing ritual that inevitably occurs whenever two dogs meet on neutral ground? Since a dog's eyesight is not very keen, and because most dogs look basically alike, he uses his sense of smell to identify other animals. As we've mentioned, a dog does not sweat and hence has no distinguishing body odor, so a curious dog has to search for distinguishing smells from the strange dog's body orifices. He picks the nonbiting end to sniff at simply because, if he has made a mistake, he'll have time to get out of the way.

You may well be asking yourself, "But if a dog's sense of smell is so keen, how can he stand to roll in dead fish or eat rotten things?" You must remember there's a distinction between *sensitivity* and *discrimination*. From a very early age, we humans are taught that certain odors are distasteful and "bad," even though they may not be actually harmful. On the other hand, a dog dislikes only those smells that mean danger or unpleasantness—such as the antiseptic smell of the vet's examining room, or the whiff of the extra secretions you automatically give off when you're mad at him. His sense of smell is probably able to find "more" in a ghastly stench than our nose can, and it's unpleasantness probably troubles him no more than an ugly shade of green would you.

A dog's sense of hearing is also particularly keen, but here he does have specific standards of what sounds are "good" or "bad." Naturally he won't care for sounds associated with things that once hurt him, or sounds heard in conjunction with obvious visual dangers. For instance, if a dog sees an elephant roaring, he will at first be terrified at the sight of the elephant itself. After that, however, the mere sound of the roaring will bring the elephant to mind, and he will be afraid of the noise too.

I worked with one dog who had an abnormal fear of the sound of a door slamming. He would run away with his tail between his legs. It turned out that as a small pup, he had been caught and hurt in a slamming door.

Notice what happens when an unusual noise crops up outside your door, especially at night. The dog senses that something is out of the ordinary, feels he is a protector, and wants to do his job. Sudden strange noises—especially footsteps—will startle him in the same way they do you. Both people and animals are frightened of the unknown. You can explain to a child what noises are, but one cannot do this with a dog. Therefore, the best approach is to expose him to strange noises and then pat him to calm his fears. This is very important when you move from the country to the city, where your dog may panic at traffic and other unaccustomed city noises.

However, no amount of familiarity will overcome a dog's inborn aversion to high-pitched noises such as a very high-pitched whistle. It's not that they are actually afraid of the sound, it's just that it annoys them, much in the same way we are bugged by fingernails scratching on a blackboard. If they can't determine the source or direction of the sound, dogs don't know which way to run and so just cry, whine, or howl.

The quality of the sound to human ears means nothing to a dog. Judy Garland was once given an Irish setter. The dog was undone by her singing and used to growl every time she revved up for a song. At one point, he actually chased her out of the room.

It's a moot point whether dogs enjoy music at all unless it relaxes *you*—in which case they are soothed by your mood, not by Beethoven. A dog's eyesight is simply too weak to help him enjoy television, and once he realizes that these human voices and images have nothing to do with him, he will usually ignore *Masterpiece Theatre*. It's the loud noises of screen violence that may bug him, but not the violence itself.

But if dogs hate whistles because of the high-pitch, why does a dog come at the sound of an "inaudible" high-pitched trainer's whistle? Simply because your dog can attach meanings to sounds quite apart from his fondness for the sound itself. He may not love the whistle, but he knows he's in trouble if he doesn't obey it.

An amusing example of how a dog uses hearing over

sight occurred when I appeared on the TV panel show *What's My Line*. I was sitting on stage, and I gave a signal for Plum to appear and promenade. The curtain opened, but Plum had disappeared. When the moderator asked me, "What does your dog do?" I told him I wasn't quite sure myself. I found out later that he had become confused by the microphone system, which made my voice sound louder at the back of the studio than at the front. Naturally, when I called him, he raced to the back, where the louder sound was coming from, knocking over a table and some sophisticated equipment en route.

Not unlike human beings, dogs need extra medical attention when young and when very old. Their relatively carefree "middle age" falls between the ages of one year and about seven or eight.

By now you should have a pretty clear picture of your dog's special canine makeup. But if you view your dog as an isolated individual, you are still far from understanding why he behaves the way he does. The entire secret of canine coexistence lies in understanding that your dog is a pack animal, constantly varying his behavior according to the company he's with. Once you understand the dynamics of pack psychology, it's remarkably easy to adapt it to your own advantage.

6 The Pack Theory

The common ancestor of both wolves and dogs was clearly a pack animal: wolves, and their close relations, jackals and dingoes, hunt in packs even today. Packs of wild dogs —or more correctly, dogs who have reverted to pack life— are an increasing problem in many suburban or rural areas. In one issue of *New York Magazine*, Dan Greenberg dramatized the wild dog situation on the Long Island shore:

> *One night last summer I was awakened by a strange sound . . . (my house in East Hampton is in a wooded area and has floor-to-ceiling windows . . .) I walked into my living room that night and there I beheld, just behind the glass, a pack of about eight German shepherds in the moonlight gazing in at me.*
>
> *I backed rapidly out of the living room and watched them watch me from the relative safety of the bedroom doorway. Eventually they slunk back into the woods to continue more pressing German shepherd activities. These dogs, I have learned, are one of a number of packs of wild dogs that roam East Hampton and other summer resort areas at night. The dogs, or their parents, were once pets which were abandoned at summer's end by their inhumane owners. The dogs have become wild and travel together for protection. They would just as soon tear out your throat as raid your garbage can.*

Before you eye your next-door neighbor's puppy as a savage marauder, we should hasten to add that Mr. Greenberg's conclusions are only partially correct. A pack

42

of wild dogs would far rather raid your garbage can than
"tear your throat out." There's no point in their taking on
a human being unless they have to—which is (a) when
there aren't enough garbage cans or local game, and
they're starving, or (b) when they see you as a dangerous
threat that has come to hunt *them*.

You can't be sure of either point, of course, because the
males who are leading the pack usually gobble the available food first, leaving the underdogs in a lean and hungry
state. Moreover, you never can be sure what constitutes a
threat to a wild dog. Had Mr. Greenberg's pack been allowed to raid garbage cans unmolested, they would probably have fled if he had stepped outside to claim his
territory. But if they had been hunted, chased, or otherwise discriminated against, they would be ready to return
the favor.

A dental assistant and her husband live in rural West-
chester, where concerted effort against a wild-dog pack
has resulted in something less than peaceful coexistence.
One night she and her husband were out with a shotgun, on the track of a garbage-raiding raccoon, when the
barking of the pack sounded from the nearby woods. Her
husband took to his heels.

"But you have a gun," she protested.

"Yeah," he panted. "But *they* don't know that."

Good point! If these dogs had been fired at before, they
would respect the sight of a shotgun, just as your own pet
is alerted by the sight of a rolled-up magazine in your
hand. But if they hadn't—or if their eyesight did not pick
up the shotgun in the dark—they would have no reserva-
tions about closing in, until it was too late for all concerned. If there is a wild pack in your locale, it can be
broken up (during daylight only), and the dogs can even
be rehabilitated. But it's best to rely on as humane methods as possible, so that whatever dogs escape remain
merely wild and not *savage*.

But a dog does not "learn" pack behavior in his master's
absence—it is built into him at birth, and a dog will revert
to pack behavior constantly, *whether he has a human master or not*. This simple fact is the key to my entire training
approach.

The male and female dog basically think and feel the
same way, except for taking on the roles that nature has
given them. In a pack situation, dogs are forced to com-

pete with one another for supremacy. Each pack is usually dominated by a single male who has proved his strength to all the other members.* Don't think that dogs are alone in their tendency to dominate the weak by force. It's a rule of behavior in every animal species, including humans!

A male dog's entire life is based on dominance—whether he's raised in the city or the country, whether or not there are other dogs present to pull rank on. *All* male dogs are born with the instinct to be a leader. Each male feels compelled to dominate—and does, while the female is generally content to let him, although females in a pack usually have a hierarchy of their own. Therefore, even after the pack leader has managed to cow the weaker males, he still must be constantly on the alert for challenges to his rule. Younger and potentially stronger males are eager to climb in the pack's hierarchy and are constantly testing their leader. In the average household, however, there is usually only one dog—who, left to himself, will assume he's the leader. If you want to be his master in more than name only, you have to convince him he's wrong—that *you* are the dominant pack leader.

Pack animals divide all other beings into two categories—leaders and followers. This is my basic training premise. When you bring a dog into your home, you inevitably become either the leader of his pack, or his follower. Training a puppy is simple because it's easy to convince him that you're stronger than he is. When he grows up, he'll still feel you can handle him easily, and is less likely to put you to any serious test.

But in any case, your show of strength can't be purely physical battle with your dog. You must use your own power of reason to overcome such basic domestication hurdles as housebreaking and obedience training. Your dog must learn to listen to your commands, such as "sit," "stay," "come," and "heel," in order to become part of the household. His species has been domesticated for so long that there really is no other place for him to go. He must learn to adjust to you as the leader.

This amazingly simple dictum could have distressing implications, however, should you consider a second dog.

Most people want a second pet to keep the current one company. When people go off to work and leave the dog alone, they become very guilty, especially if their dog is a

---

* In some cases, a dominant female will emerge as pack leader.

young one, and decide to get it a playmate. They also think that the extra dog will make the training procedures go easier. But obviously, once you have more than one dog in the house, you have what constitutes the basis of a pack.

Those who claim that the first dog will be less messy, destructive, and lonely with a second dog, are mistaken. Two of anything can be better or worse than one of anything, simply because one of your dogs will immediately accept the other one as dominant. If he is paying full attention to his canine pack leader, you may wind up being ignored completely.

What if you already have one dog in his prime, and then introduce another dog to your household? If the newcomer is a puppy, you have little cause to worry—he'll automatically accept the older dog as his superior. But if you are introducing two males of approximately the same age, chances are they will fight unless you are in complete control—unless, that is, both dogs respect your authority and ability to give them orders.

One suburban matron keeps twelve German shepherds with her at all times. They simply stay around the house, wandering from room to room of her large house. She employs lots of help to assist with the dogs, but she never really gets involved in their training– which presents a big problem. I've been able to train only three of them with any satisfaction. The woman does not give the whole matter enough time, there's no one *person* the dogs can identify as their leader. She simply likes the idea of having a dozen dogs crowding around her, but as time goes by, whatever dominant male is in control of the pack will eventually detrain the three animals that I have managed to reach.

Remember the perfectly housebroken Maltese who urinated on the editor's foot back in chapter 1? He was the dominant male in the "pack" his owner created when she brought home the second Maltese. But it wasn't that the new, younger dog detrained him. Rather, his position of dominance gave him new self-confidence, to the point where he decided to test his mistress's rules. The second Maltese then followed his cue.

For this reason, removing the dominant male can often have a quieting effect on the rest of a pack. Two males, from the same litter had a habit of putting other neighborhood dogs in the hospital, one by one. When the larger, more aggressive male developed kidney problems and was put to sleep, he was no longer there to incite his brother to aggressive action. The surviving dog relaxed, literally overnight.

But in any case, it's easy for *any* dog in your private pack to get out of line simply because of the presence of another dog. Therefore, training of one and training of two must necessarily be a little different. When training two dogs in the house it is best to work thoroughly with one alone, and then the other—alone also. When you are successful in that area, then work with them both.

A good example of this type of training took place when I was called in to direct the canines in Robert Downey's *Pound*—to be exact, forty dogs and a cat! (In one scene that quickly hit the cutting-room floor, a zealous dog mounted an unsuspecting cat, while a Great Dane's legs were simultaneously mounted by four terriers.) For *Pound,* I had to train them all to live amicably together. To do this I had to construct a pack of which I was the leader.

How? Not easy. I started by bringing in the pups first and working with them, then with the females both young and old. Females will fight if left alone, but are easier to control if there is a dominant male around. These females would get obnoxious once in a while, but they were easier to control than males.

After that I worked with the young adult males alone, got their respect through dominance. Two of them assumed leadership over the other males, so I made sure these two were on a leash when I introduced the males to the pack of females and pups. As soon as they seemed to be pretty well integrated, I released one of the aggressive young males. Each time he got a little nasty, I reprimanded him and persisted until he stopped. I then repeated the same procedure with the second young aggressive male.

As long as I was there, everything was peaceful. But if I left, I had to tie the two young males up, because once I did leave for about a minute, and they started fighting in an attempt to assume leadership. This fight would have been extremely bloody—so strong is their instinct to lead. Fortunately they didn't have enough time to really get into it.

I used young dogs to keep the chance of fighting to a minimum, but since each dog in the movie had to be a representative of a particular breed—and that breed in turn was representative of a human counterpart—I also had to use a seven-year-old sixty pound Mexican hairless and a six-year-old English bulldog. These two dogs were never allowed out of sight for a second. They were both completely untrustworthy. Both also wanted to lead.

My assistant was always within two feet of the bulldog and I within the same distance of the hairless. We each carried a blanket, and every time a dog looked as if he might get into a battle, a blanket was thrown over him, and he was pulled away. Each of these two dogs were worked with separately for two weeks before being introduced to the pack. This quarantine period was used to make sure that the dogs responded instantly to commands given either by myself or my assistant. Even so they were never trustworthy and were used only when absolutely necessary.

I used the same principle when introducing the cat. He was first put in with the pups, then with the young females, later with the young males, and finally with the dominant males. Any dog who attempted to bother him was discouraged immediately. Eventually he was accepted. In fact, he sort of got lost amongst the dogs.

I take Plum with me whenever I visit a client for training. For one thing, it gives the owners an incentive to work with their own dogs. Once they see what a well-trained dog is like, they want to have one too. It gives them a goal. I also use Plum as an example for what I expect the other dog to do and put him through an exercise for the owners. It is much easier to demonstrate than to explain what I want done.

But at the same time, I use Plum's dominant instincts to an advantage. Dogs relate to other dogs and pick up habits, good and bad, from one another; all dogs respond to a dominant leader. When dogs see Plum responding to me, they have an instinctive tendency to do likewise. This doesn't mean that the client's dog will automatically listen to me, but it does give me a starting point.

Sheepdog puppies are sent out with the older, more experienced dogs to learn to herd sheep. Once they've picked up the basics, their trainers give them additional technical pointers to make them really good at it. I use this same principle.

However, training by a human—me, that is—finishes off the job, so don't expect your neighbor's well-trained dog to train yours. He can help set an example, but you must do the teaching.

On the other hand, another dog can be the main reason for disobedience on the part of your pet. So later in the training, I use Plum as a distraction to the dog I am working with, so that the owner can be sure his pet will always respond, even when there are other dogs around. For example, I have the owner make his dog sit and stay, then I send Plum over to annoy him. The dog sees another of his own kind and naturally wants to be with him, but he must be taught to do what *you* want and not what *he* wants. If the dog still sits after Plum goes over to him, I can be pretty confident that he's listening to his owner.

7 Other Facets
of Pack Behavior

In or out of a pack situation, a dog uses his urine to establish his territory.* As we've seen, a dog's skin has no pores, and thus he has no distinctive body odor all his own. However, his nose is acutely sensitive to acid— and uric acid, of course, is a main ingredient in any animal's urine. No two dogs' urine smells are the same.

The acid eats into whatever it touches, and is thus a more or less permanent marker—which any dog can distinguish months or even up to a year later, despite the actions of soap, wind, or weather. Naturally the intensity of the smell diminishes in time, so that the intensity of the scent is a good "clock," telling any dog how recently another male has passed that way.

That is why, once outside, your dog's first act is to smell all of the local fire hydrants, lamp posts, or trees. If you watch him carefully, you'll find that he often goes in exactly the same spots. This is because he wants to cover the smell of a dog who's already been by, to reaffirm his presence.

One owner complained to me that when he and his dog visited Fire Island, his animal forgot all about being housebroken. He and the other dogs present must have lifted their leg a thousand times indoors. In this case, territorial instinct simply overcame training: the dogs were marking off their territory this way, especially since it was a new place. But even on a dogless street, a dog will spray the same corner or tree day after day for the same reason

---
* Understanding this simple behavior pattern is vital to housebreaking your dog effectively, which we'll discuss in a later chapter.

that authors renew their copyrights on books—to keep
the odor strong enough so that the territory does not
lapse into "public domain."

The next time you take your dog along on a picnic,
you'll see a good example of how he uses his urine to
establish his territory. Once you have set out your blanket
and food and settled down, your dog will usually move in
a circle around the blanket, pausing to lift his leg here
and there. This establishes his fighting perimeter. Any
dog who approaches his urine-marked area will get a
growl or bark.

If your dog still feels his territory threatened, he will begin walking in a circle around the area he feels driven to
protect. If the "new" dog heeds this warning, he will either
retreat or accept dominance. If he doesn't, the defending
dog will then escalate to a higher form of warning—a leg
lift on a spot near the invader. If the invader wants to
challenge the other, he will then urinate on the same spot,
and the two of them will usually alternate as in the chil-

FIGHT

WATCH

IGNORE

dren's game of "Said It Last." Finally, one dog will either get tired of these shenanigans, back down, or chase the other away.

Should the other dog step inside the original circle, your dog will fight. He'll usually win, because a dog who feels territorially justified will attack with absolutely no fear, and fight with 100 percent of his capacity. An invader *knows* he's intruding, simply by the smell of urine, and he will usually fight halfheartedly, like a soldier sent to defend a foreign country.

But as long as other dogs stay well outside that acrid line, your dog won't care and may even ignore them. The exception occurs when the owner of the land has a dog who already considers the whole meadow as his range and won't acknowledge any claim jumpers.

Once out of the house a mature male urinates constantly in small amounts. He will never completely empty his bladder, always saving some urine for later use. It may be that a male's partly full bladder even gives him a feeling of confidence. In fact a mature male uses both feces and urine to establish his territory. My dog often defecates many times even during a short walk.

Most mammals, and even man in some cases, employ their own excrement in an aggressive fashion. My little Maltese, Inches, was too small to take on Plum personally, so he would defecate right next to the Weimaraner's food dish, kick out his four legs, and trot off victoriously. I have to remind many a client that when a dog urinates near, or on, a human being, it's not simply a question of housebreaking. The dog is showing his aggression and dominance over his human counterparts.

One dog belonging to a family of children directed by a nanny would relieve himself only in the bedsheets—probably because nanny was so used to covering up the kids' lapses in toilet training that she concealed the dog's misbehavior too; but also because he felt he owned the children and was letting them know it by adding his own territorial claims. By keeping the dog confined in the same room with one adult member of the family at night, they gradually coaxed him to the outside.

You must remember that a dog is constantly testing his pack leader—or in other words, you. In the wild he fights for survival. In the home everything is taken care of for him—so he spends the whole day thinking up ways to get *more* of what is enjoyable for him. He is always looking to dominate.

For example, one perfectly innocent young couple was sabotaged by what they thought was going to be a fun pet. They decided to buy a dog for all of the standard reasons, and since they had never had experience with a dog before, spent hours reading about his care. The book education they looked into concerned training and talking to the dog communicatively. Not too much stress was put on discipline.

The two tried so very hard to be loving masters that the first signs of the dog's taking over were not noticed. They loved their dog, so they looked the other way. They would clean up the dog's messes and say "no," but these were not "no's" with any kind of authority or vigor. When the dog chewed up their antique bed, they simply locked him out of the bedroom. Being human, they often neglected to close the door, so once again the dog could chew on their belongings to his heart's content.

They did worry about their valuable hand-carved Chinese furniture, however, which they stashed away in one of the smaller rooms of their five-room apartment. The TV followed. Anything they really cherished was confined to this dog-free sanctuary. Friends and neighbors began touching on the subject, and finally one of the prisoners decided to fight back. When he reprimanded the animal for messing on the Oriental rug, the dog growled at him. He called the dog's bluff, the dog bit him, and he called his vet in a panic. The doctor told him to call me.

He called and explained what had happened. I recognized the situation immediately and instructed him to leave the phone off the hook, go get the dog and firmly reprimand him.

He was hesitant, but I told him that he *must* correct the dog immediately, or he could well have a biting dog on his hands.

If a dog isn't stopped on the first bite, chances are he'll try again. You can't let a dog dominate you. You must be the authority or he will take over.

You'll notice that your dog doesn't like to maintain eye contact, especially if you don't show any emotion but just stare. To a dog, staring is an aggressive act, just like the game played between two people who try to outstare each other. If two dogs are staring at each other, eventually one will always look away, and this in itself is a sign of defeat. If you stare at a full-grown male you do not know, he will probably growl, bark, or possibly even attempt to defend himself in some way.

If you are going to give your dog any hand or voice commands, do not continue staring at him after he's carried out your wishes, since he'll take your stare as a sign of displeasure. And if you must stare at your dog, be sure to give him a command at the same time—otherwise you will confuse him. But you can use the "stare test" to determine if your dog accepts you as boss, simply by the length of time it takes him to avert his gaze from yours.

You must be equally alert to what it means when your dog stares at *you*—such as when you're at the dinner table. If you finally give him a tidbit off your plate, he thinks *you* are the submissive one. You did what he wanted, didn't you? Whenever a dog stares at you, he wants you to submit to his present whim—to go out, eat, sleep on your bed, or be patted.

Just as your dog has specific signs like leg-lifting for challenging his pack leader, so he has other specific gestures to indicate that he'll toe the line. When an errant pet gets smacked with a rolled newspaper, by way of a reprimand, he will often crawl down on all fours or roll over on his back with his feet in the air. This is a submissive reaction. Rolling over is his way of giving in, admitting that he accepts your superiority.

The whole point of these stylized urinations, staring, and submissive gestures is to avoid the necessity of actual physical battle. Without the ability to challenge—and defeat—each other through these harmless "games," pack animals would be forced to attack each other at the slightest provocation, and the species would quickly be exterminated.

This "ritualized behavior" is the key to disciplining your dog *without* the use of actual physical force. A puppy quickly learns that you're bigger and stronger than he is, but once he's grown up, why does he fall in line at a slight tap with a rolled newspaper? Depending on his size, it may not even be painful, but it's the concept of your disfavor that undoes him. If he accepts you as his pack leader, his main drive, between periods of testing you, will be to do things that earn your approval.

In the next chapter, we'll begin to explore precisely *how* he determines what's expected of him.

8 Between Human and Dog

Konrad Lorenz, who has unravelled the behavior patterns of jackdaws, geese, water shrews, and stickleback fish, was once baffled by his own dog! In his classic *King Solomon's Ring,* he admits:

> *My Alsatian, Tito, knew by "telepathy" exactly which people got on my nerves, and when. Nothing could prevent her from biting, gently but surely, all such people on their posteriors. It was particularly dangerous for authoritative old gentlemen to adopt towards me the well-known "you are, of course, too young" attitude. No sooner had the stranger thus expostulated, than his hand felt anxiously for the place in which Tito had punctiliously chastised him. I could never understand how it was that this reaction functioned just as reliably when the dog was lying under the table and was therefore precluded from seeing the faces and gestures of the people round it: how did she know who I was speaking to or arguing with?*

With what you now know of a dog's senses, the answer ought to be obvious. The dog could *not see* whom Lorenz was arguing with, but she could listen and, of course, smell. Scent and hearing are all a dog needs to judge *your* mood and locate *your* source of antagonism. A dog knows instinctively that he must please his leader, so the tone of your voice is often enough to make a well-trained dog respond to you.

But after you have had your dog for a while, he also knows exactly what the smell of your body chemistry is.

He can sense any changes in it, because if you are afraid, angry, or excited, your adrenal glands work overtime and your body gives off extra sweat through the pores in your skin. The dog's sense of smell is so acute that he picks up this change in your odor and responds accordingly.

A dentist once told me, "My dog only barks at mean-looking characters, such as long-haired hippies or black people." I asked him how he felt about these people himself. It turned out that he felt frightened when they walked near him. The dog was only picking up his master's unspoken reaction.

This helps explain Konrad Lorenz's mystery—but how did Tito know *which* guest to bite? A dog can pick up the reactions of other people as well as his master and will, again, act accordingly. Tito could easily hear the "too young" attitude in the words of any "authoritative old gentleman"—not necessarily the words, but the tone of voice.

A dog understands only a limited number of words, and unless conversation is directed specifically at him, he will probably not react to any words except his name and such promising concepts as "out," "ride," or "food." Like his master, a dog reacts only to what concerns him; the rest bores him. And so, dogs quickly learn to respond to your tone of voice, because they can easily use it as an index to your pleasure or anger. To prove this quickly, praise your dog in a stern, harsh voice and watch his tail and ears droop. Then really chew him out in happy, loving tones, and see the transformation. Of course, if your voice is a habitual grumble, they'll learn to love that, and react to pats and food rather than wait for a "happy" tone of voice.

The reason a dog sees your "enemies" as his is because he accepts you as his pack leader. It is true that a dominant male dog will test you constantly to try to become pack leader himself, but the threat of danger to you will temporarily suppress even *his* feeling of competition toward you, and he will rally wholeheartedly to the "pack's" defense.

When someone who is frightened of dogs comes to visit you, the dog can sense this right off from the increased odor. If you are friendly toward your frightened guest, your dog's natural dominant instincts will often translate themselves into excessive attention, hence the perennial complaint, "I don't like dogs. Then why do they always come around me?" The answer is to test you out, to see if you'll accept them as dominant over you. But if their owners weren't around to set a good example, their attention might be of a different sort.

Dogs really do know when you're scared, and when *you know* they know, it's doubly hard to remain cool. You can be around a friend and his dogs for weeks, only to find the dogs regard you as any other suspicious character the moment you're apart from their master. Once a house guest of mine was gathering her clothes and various paraphernalia out of bureau drawers. I had gone out to the corner delicatessen, and in my absence the dogs decided she was some kind of intruder, taking things that didn't belong to her. She received a few warning growls and decided it would be better to pack when I returned.

If you plan to continue a social existence populated by varying numbers of other humans, you *must* train your dog about strangers and insist that he treat them with utmost courtesy. Otherwise, he's apt to "read" your scent

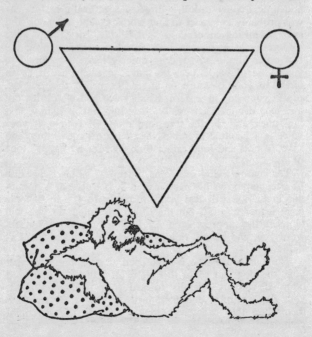

some day and treat your mother-in-law the way *you'd* really like to.

There exists a situation with the same dynamics as a human love triangle, only in this case one of the members is a dog. Oftentimes, when a person living alone owns a dog, the dog assumes an equal position in the house. Then, when another person enters the picture, a problem often develops. The dog may feel his secure position is jeopardized and will act accordingly. He may become hostile toward the new person or annoying to his owner in an attempt to regain all the attention and affection.

One of my clients had this problem. At first her dog just growled at her dates when they came to visit her, and she just laughed it off as a joke. Then one day the dog bit one of them. After that, before inviting dates to her house, she had to make sure that they weren't afraid of dogs. Eventually, however, she couldn't invite *anyone*, because her dog had become too aggressive to control. She couldn't understand why.

The first thing I did was to explain the "love triangle syndrome" to her. I told her that if the dog wasn't stopped immediately, it would always be just her alone with her dog.

The only way to correct this problem is to reprimand your dog whenever he gets out of hand. This is the kindest thing you can do because most of the people who can't control this problem give their dogs away, and who knows where they end up?

Many people feel that this whole phenomenon is simply the result of disillusionment at having lost the center of attention. It is *not*, however, and should be treated merely as an aggressive act on the dog's part. If you make the mistake of paying a little extra attention to your dog to make up for his feeling displaced, you are letting yourself in for plenty of trouble. He will think that he is being praised for his aggression, and it will only become more overt. So please remember, it's the reprimand that will straighten this out, *not* feeling sorry.

In the case of the newlyweds, it is the dog's original owner who must correct the situation and make sure the dog is not aggressive. The new person in the house cannot immediately punish the dog for an aggressive act because the punishment will have no meaning and could quite easily make the dog resent him/her. If the dog's aggression is ended immediately, he should soon accept the new family member.

If you want your dog to get along with children, it's important that he'd been around humans since his puppyhood and been handled a great deal. Dogs often bite out of fear. You can assuage this problem before it starts by making sure he's used to people.

You can put a baby on the floor next to a puppy. Don't be afraid, but do stick around. The baby will be left intact. A dog catches on miraculously fast that children are his friends, as long as someone takes the time to introduce them properly. Many times the good behavior potential of kids and animals alike is just wasted because no one takes the time to explore and develop it.

Obviously, you should keep children segregated from strange dogs, whose previous training, temperament, and habits are not known to you. But family dogs that have not been attack-trained will never bother children in a family, unless there are extraordinary circumstances. For instance, running children can be exciting to a dog. He may run after them, playfully nipping or jumping at them without meaning to hurt them. But if the children panic, the dog can then become aggressive. Therefore, it is extremely important that these habits be curbed by obedience training.

If a small child is caught in the melee between two males fighting over a female in heat, things can get dangerous, especially if he cries and shows obvious signs of panic. Therefore, also remember to teach your child how to behave around dogs.

A problem could develop when the dog belongs to the family first. A newborn baby can disillusion a dog who used to get enormous amounts of attention from his masters. One dog became so upset about being pushed out of a central position by the new baby that one day, while the baby was in the playpen, he jumped into the baby's crib. I had to sit the family down and explain what was going on.

The thing to do, again, is to try to get the dog used to children. When the dog comes near the child, don't panic. Don't explain to him that he is not being forgotten, because the more attention he gets, the worse the situation will become. Just quietly chase him away *if* you don't want him around the child. Eventually the dog and baby will become good friends. Most of the time when you hear of dogs being jealous of children, it's conjured up in the minds of the people telling the story. An animal will accept his environment.

Parents with more than one child often get a dog for each child to relieve arguments of whose dog it is. Generally this arrangement works out until the first feeding time comes around, and the responsibility falls on the parents. I have to laugh when people reminisce about the fun they had caring for their dogs when they were little. Most kids never really do take care of the dogs. The chores of dogdom usually are handled by parents.

If you have very young children, though, any dog you get should grow to be a sizeable animal. I find something unsettling about seeing a small dog in a house with small children. The child looms up over a small animal and is more likely to hurt it than it would a larger dog.

Psychological transference is one of the most fascinating aspects of the animal behavior problems I deal with. Surely you know families with whiny children whose dogs whine just as annoyingly, the single girl whose dog picks up ten men per day, the ranting movie star whose dog barks and generally tears up the place.

When I ask a client what it is about his dog that he doesn't like, the answer is usually some habit the dog picked up from his master.

If you placed a brand-new dog in a standard household, in less than six months he would come out bearing all of the psychological traits of the family itself. A dog comes into your family world like a clean blackboard, and whatever you do *must* influence him. Where else can he pick it up?

This is not to say that the dog becomes *exactly* what his master is. Instead, the dog of a nervous owner—for example—quickly learns to cater to his master's paranoia at every squeak and rattle after dark. By following what he feels is expected of him, the dog then *appears* nervous. The owner then assumes that he has a neurotic dog, but don't forget a dog's not complex enough to develop neurosis. His prime drives are for territory, sex, food, and self-preservation. When people get involved in training their dogs, they should give up their grade-school psychology.

Often an owner decides that his dog must be jealous

when he's petting another dog, and his own dog pushes the newcomer out of the way. But in no way is this jealousy. Prove this by throwing out a piece of food in the direction of the "jealous" dog. If he were truly jealous, he'd let the other dog grab the food and bask in your affection. But in reality, he'll leave you and the competing dog alone and race for the food. Jealousy is in your mind, not his. When there's a lot of free affection being given out, he's just making sure he gets his share, but the prospect of food will chase any such worries out of his mind.

Dogs learn to take full advantage of all your weaknesses. My dog once broke his leg in a fight with a malamute. After the cast was removed from his leg, he continued to limp. Naturally I was especially affectionate toward him, watching out for him and making sure he had comfortable places to lie. Months later, although the veterinarian said the bone had healed perfectly he was still favoring that leg.

One day while walking him, I stopped in front of a glazier's window and glanced into one of the display mirrors and caught sight of more than just my own image. There, reflected in the mirror, was Plum, my dog, walking along with a completely normal gait—now that he felt safely out of my line of vision.

Dog owners must be taught how important every move with the dog can be. *You* are the reason your dog does most things right or wrong. You probably couldn't remember how you taught your dog half the things he knows. When you bring a puppy home at six weeks of age, he *has* to pick up habits, both good and bad. What most people don't realize is that your dog is *always* responding to you, even when you're ignoring him. Even if you're not "teaching" your dog, he'll be learning things on his own.

If a puppy is put into a car and taken to the vet for his shots, he may associate going for shots with getting into the car, and be reluctant to travel by auto ever after.

One puppy, coming out of the elevator, was startled when a delivery man dropped a heavy crate right beside the door. The dog had to be forcibly pulled from the elevator every time thereafter, having been convinced that a crate would fall every time he left an elevator.

Be very careful about what human attributes you give your dog, because you're going to have to live with them. One matronly lady deposits her dog in the kennel when she travels, instructing the kennel keeper that her pet must have his favorite blanket with him at all times, that he's crazy without his pet toy. It *is* good for a dog to have one familiar object around while he's being boarded, but in reality, her dog would be fine without the paraphernalia. It's just that he realized that he got more attention when he played with what she thought were his favorite toys.

It's vital for you to realize that you are the one who sets the habit patterns for your dog. If you approve of his habits, great, but later if you decide that what he's doing is not up to your standards, the damage is already done. You'll have to break the habit that you set up for him.

The same predicament is true of sleeping arrangements. One insecure Maltese was recovering from an illness and was allowed to sleep in his mistress's bed. To this day, the dog is still snuggled in with her. Why should he sleep somewhere else if he's got this whole big bed to luxuriate in?

A dog is very much like a human in one respect. He wants and will take as much as he can possibly get out of life. And so, if you take your dog to bed because he's so very cute and wonderful, you'd better decide you want him with you forever, right there on your bed. Better yet, soon he'll decide he wants to be tucked under the blankets. He may even push you to one end of the bed while he controls the rest of it.

When you give your dog what he wants to shut him up, you're really setting yourself up for years of spoiled dogdom. If he learns that by growling or biting he can keep whatever he has ill-gotten, you might very well have a biter on your hands. If he figures you'll let him out whenever he scratches at the door, he'll scratch twenty times per day. I can point out at least a hundred examples of people who are slaves to their dog's whim to bail out in the middle of the night. The dog whines, and they are dressed in a flash.

Your dog may be your pal, but what pal controls your every move? You should have learned by now that your dog waits for you, that he is under your control. You don't have to come to love *his* way of life—unless you want to.

Part Two

BASIC CARE
AND
CONTROLLING
BAD HABITS

9 Where Dog Owners Go Wrong

It's rewarding to pay close attention to how your friends, and the dog owners mentioned in this book, handle their dog problems. You can learn more from studying their mistakes than from any training manual.

I can't see a time when all dogs will be trained. There are just too many dog owners who don't understand the advantages of training and find it hard to believe that they do not have complete control over their animals. A vast majority think they can do it, just like their fathers before them, and stop right there.

In training dogs, often the main chore for me is training the owners. From being around thousands of dogs, I understand how they work and know that, with the proper patience and understanding, their problems can be solved. My clients do not have the same confidence I have because they haven't had the experience. One wealthy couple, very spoiled in the luxuries of life, spent my initial visits complaining about how difficult it was to train their dog. I asked them how long they had been going to their psychiatrist. "About five years," was their answer.

Just like anything worthwhile, proper training takes more than an average amount of patience, plus a strong desire to do a really good job.

No halfhearted pet owners can achieve the ultimate in pet relationships. This is an axiom not all dog owners are happy to grasp. Some don't relate to dogs as animals but rather as a luxury item such as a car or a new fur coat. Oftentimes they pick the most exotic and expensive breed merely to display it as a status symbol.

One mysterious caller with a foreign accent refused to

leave her name or number, just kept saying she was a private secretary and that she would call back. And each time she did, it was a different breed of dog she claimed she wanted trained. Eventually she confessed that the dog really belonged to her employer (a gilt-edged celebrity whose wealth has made her name a household word). The lady simply did not want anyone to know what kind of dog she had, lest it be kidnapped when the professional dogwalkers picked it up in the lobby of her Fifth Avenue apartment building. Tight security was needed to keep the dog's identity out of the newspapers.

I put a stop to the calls by suggesting Mrs. ———— should hire someone else. I told her to tell her "busy" and "famous" employer that it was obvious that she was not interested in her dog. And that apparently she thinks of him as a toy, a book, or clothing from a department store. People who want well-trained dogs must work at it.

I still get angry when I think of the uncle who bought a dog for his spoiled nephew. The uncle paid the pet shop for a Siberian husky but told the manager to hold the dog until his nephew could come by to see it. Later he appeared with his nephew, who fell for the dog at once. The store owner was then ordered to hold the dog for a couple of weeks more until the boy's parents were convinced that they really needed a dog. The aforesaid parents knew nothing of the joy of a pet dog—just what they heard on the late-night shows about the problems of maintenance and harassment. So the dog was kept on hold for several weeks, like a piece of shelved luggage.

Complications developed when the uncle purchased his nephew three pet gerbils. The boy already had a matched set of snakes, and couldn't handle the new rush of animals, so he asked his uncle to deposit the snakes "at that nice store where they're keeping my husky."

Vacation time came around, and the entire menagerie was boarded out to the pet shop. Nothing was said about the daily increasing age of the animals, or the fact that an older, untrained husky could play havoc with human beings. As far as I know the animals are still there. This family has no idea of the love and affection surrounding the whole concept of pets.

I can't understand how so many people go through the motions of having a dog, but don't really want to give it love. I once bought a collie that was being cruelly treated by his owner, kicked, beaten, often locked in the bathroom for days, and gave it to a deserving owner. Not all people are worthy of pets. Animals are entrusted to us, they are special creatures and people have to earn their right to a dog, for there is a lot of care and affection involved.

Still, many of the people who hire me merely want to be able to tell their friends how expensive their dog's analyst is. When they call me, they expect me to train their dog in much the same way as a mechanic would fix a car. A prospective client once offered me several thousand dollars to make his dog perfect. I turned him down just as I would turn down anyone I didn't think capable of the mammoth job of maintaining an animal. If anyone wants the perfect dog, he is the one who must train him and not me. I assign my clients certain exercises I expect them to follow. I can't do these for them because I don't live with them. I can only advise and consult. In the final analysis it is the owner who must take on the sizable responsibility of training his dog.

Don't get the impression that this problem exists only with the idle rich; it is just as prevalent among average working persons. Any unsuccessful training I might have had has been with people who cannot accept the fact that they must work at having a well-trained animal.

My biggest hurdle in getting my work done effectively is that many dog owners don't really listen. At first, they usually find me entertaining and don't take their pets' training seriously enough. It usually takes me three to four weeks, and longer in some cases, just to dog-orient these people and make them realize that their animal is alive. If clients would listen to me the very first time, I could save them weeks of training, but for the first few weeks they do not follow my lessons. So, the only one who has ever worked with the dog is me, and therefore the dog will usually respond only to me.

On about the third or fourth lesson these clients inform me that the training is not working and that the dog isn't responding at all. So, since it takes only a little while to teach the most basic obedience commands, I put the dog through his paces, and he does everything perfectly.

This is usually the turning point. Clients then realize that the dog can and does respond, and they want him to do it for *them*. Now they want not only the best-looking dog but also the best-trained dog. This concept is very exciting to them, and only now can we get down to the business of training the dog in earnest.

After three months of concentrated effort on getting her dog to obey promptly, an eminent female psychiatrist confided to me, "You really do know what you're doing. When I listen to what you say and do it, my dog behaves perfectly, responds to my every command."

I have seen some remarkable changes in attitude on the part of many of these people, but it's an extremely difficult thing to accomplish. Sometimes I have to find out what they dislike about dogs and cover that training area first.

Dogs don't respond to people who are busy doing other things while trying to train them. How can you teach your dog to sit while chatting with a friend over your child's progress in school? Training takes your full attention. You need the time to learn about your dog, just as he needs a while to learn your laws. One well-trained dog even regressed to his original behavior, because his owner's business expanded, leaving him little or no time for the lonely dog. I always tell people that if they own a pet, they must be able to give him time and love.

Intelligence and education have nothing to do with the level on which you relate to your dog. The psychiatrist I just mentioned is a brilliant woman who deals with scores of people every day on a high level of communication. However, when it comes to dealing with her dog, she is an absolute failure. Training is *not* an intellectual matter. It is plain and simple discipline. I use the same methods for third graders as I do for Ph.D.s. It's just that the third graders learn faster. The more intellectual the person, the more he looks for this whole process to be complicated.

One dog owner with two Great Danes told me he didn't believe in training at all, he held that all dogs do the proper thing because they love you. "You just talk nice to them." However, this man was a union organizer, used to handling people in a firm, decisive way. He never lost his temper, but just kept plodding until he got what he wanted. What dog wouldn't respond to that approach? He spent hours getting his dogs to do such things as relieving themselves outside "out of love." What he was actually doing—despite all his talk about love—was training his dogs. He was doing exactly what I do, only he put a big "love" label on it. I love dogs too.

Many people have unusual ways of getting their dogs to obey. One woman, whose dog is now part of my training program, spent too much time commanding her dog to do things: "Fritz, I told you no. If I told you once, I told you a thousand times, never, ever, chew my shoes."

Why should a dog have to listen to all of this? Chances are he won't. And if he does obey, it will actually be because of the word "no," possibly the word "shoe," but most certainly his owner's persistence.

Commands shouldn't be lengthy, verbose chains of words which will only confuse an animal. Just a single word is enough. Your dog can perform virtually all of the exercises and tricks explained later in this book simply by hearing a one-word command. If you prefer saying "go get the ball" rather than "fetch," it's because the phrase may be easier for *you* to remember. When I work with children, I find them much easier to train than their parents. They usually call me Paul on first contact, but in the next few visits they are impressed enough to begin addressing me as Mr. Loeb. And I have to tell them it's all right to call me Paul. They really listen and assimilate, while their parents often just put in time, thinking that's all that is necessary.

Many children who are afraid of dogs got that way because of their parents. One thirty-five-year-old woman, who had been told by her mother that dogs are vicious, never quite got over that notion, but somehow her husband talked her into getting a dog. When she answered the door on my first visit, her dog growled at Plum, who reciprocated. In a state of instinctive shock, the woman slammed the door on all three of us. (Now that she knows what makes dogs the way they are, she has a well-trained cocker.)

One child in the East 50's plays very roughly with a sheepdog. They run, play, and generally get tangled up in one another, but the child's father is terrified of the dog and spends days warning his son that he will get bitten.

Children don't pick up fear of dogs from their playmates or from experience. It's the fear and nervousness in Mom and Dad that teach a child that there is something to watch out for.

I make a real effort to counteract such parental propaganda. Whenever children seem nervous around Plum, I jokingly tell them, "Don't bite my dog." This seems to calm their fears and at the same time it gives their mothers confidence, too, even the ones who are at first apprehensive about Plum.

A schoolteacher whose dog I worked with asked me to speak to her students on animal behavior and dog training. Before the lecture date, I thoroughly prepared myself for an interesting morning with some twelve-to fourteen-year-olds at summer school and even organized some notes on what topics I would cover. I arrived to find that I had been given the address of a day camp. I went in anyway, and was greeted by a most active group of five-year-olds who were obviously ready for me. Before I could say a word, they had colored a picture of my dog with the brightest shades of paint imaginable and had bombarded me with such good, meaty questions as "Is Plum a mommy or a daddy?"

I answered as best I could, crumpled up my prepared speech on animal training, joined them on the floor, and had a good time. Kids *naturally* love animals, without fear or worry, and often it's best to follow their example.

10 Reprimands: the Word "No" and Body Language

At one apartment, I spent weeks trying to stop the dog from chewing the table. "What on earth can we do to stop this?" the mother asked. Her two-year-old baby looked at me and answered, "Tell him no."

I can't overstress the need for explaining *simply* to your dog what you require of him. One schoolteacher spent an entire Sunday afternoon planting a houseful of greenery while her trusty beagle sat around watching her. It looked like great fun, so when she went out for the evening, he replanted—and nibbled—everything. When she called me in despair on Monday morning, I predicted that all of her beagle's problems would soon be over if her dog ever sampled her poisonous Dieffenbachia. I then asked her to relate exactly what had gone on while she was planting.

According to her, she had *told* her dog not to sniff around the flowers because it would upset them, and she gave him a cookie for listening to her, or so she thought. But that cookie was her mistake! The beagle decided that the cookie was a reward, that she *liked* him hanging around the flowers. So why was she so furious when she returned to see all of the nice work that he had done?

It's all communication. You must let your dog know what you want. "No," or even a mild slap, is better communication than the anger the schoolteacher let loose on her poor beagle when she saw the mess. She kicked him and screamed hysterically. To avoid this whole scene, she should have simply said "no," when he sniffed the plants, and he would have known in no uncertain way that they were off limits to him.

I told her to take her dog over to the plants, and not to touch the pot until the dog did something overt about eating the plant. As soon as he went for a plant, she was to slap his muzzle and say "no" emphatically.

I often find it difficult to get owners to reprimand their dogs because they don't like to be "unpleasant." In addition, "discipline" seems like a dirty word to many people, because it makes them think of all the things they should be doing themselves. Walking, feeding, and training your dog often brings to mind all of the exercising and dieting habits human beings should be following.

The word "no" literally covers a multitude of sins. It's the one word—really the *only* word—an owner ever needs in the way of a reprimand. Perhaps your dog has a habit of taking his leash and running with it. A firm "no" at the first sign of this will usually end it right away. When you have company, stop to consider whose company it is, yours or your dog's. Visitors provide new smells, new sounds, and enough affection to make any dog overexcited. It will take at least five minutes to enforce your sit/stay orders, whereas a firm "no" will calm the dog down to a level of peaceful coexistence.

Try to maintain a standard mood with your dog. When you grouse around the house within earshot of your dog, he'll most likely do what you request or stay out of your way. But if you are in a really good mood, most likely you're far more lenient and forgiving.

A capital rule is to correct any bad habit promptly. If you haven't got time to scold him right now, and you decide to forget it just this once, congratulations! You have just won yourself a dog who won't listen to a word you say. It's the "just onces" that will ruin the master/dog relationship.

"No" should be the only word used to correct your dog, since it's a reprimand not a command. And remind yourself not to be mean after the dog is reprimanded. There's no point in "punishing" your dog by locking him in the bathroom for three or four hours. After a few minutes, he probably won't remember what he was being punished for. All you are doing by this is teaching the dog to stay in the bathroom. He thinks he's simply in another room, and since most dogs will accept whatever situation they are given, if they have no choice, he'll just hang out there till you come get him. Instead, after saying the harsh "no," turn around and walk away. Then just leave him alone for five or ten minutes.

Whenever you take a bad habit away from a dog, you must replace it with a good one. This small point can be the difference in whether or not your dog is trained properly. When you explain to a child not to cough in people's faces, you also demonstrate coughing into a handkerchief. Do the same thing with dog training. When you say "no," be sure that a short time (about ten minutes) later, you also show him what's right. If he's not allowed to sit on the couch, where *can* he sit? Over there in his corner. Put him there and praise him for being obedient. This way, he'll learn the difference between right and wrong. Dogs need affection. They have to feel loved at all times. Otherwise punishment doesn't have much meaning. So, a short while after reprimanding your dog, give him a command and praise him for doing it properly.

We've already seen that a dog's hearing is better than his sight. But nevertheless, I believe that you should use hand commands along with words from the very start. A puppy will respond to hand commands faster than to words, because body language (motion) is a dog's own way of communication. If you watch a mother with her pups, you will see that she doesn't attempt to bark commands, but instead uses direct physical means. She pushes, points, nudges, and pulls. This is what the puppies understand. Therefore hand commands are the best, simplest, and most direct way that a human can work so as to be on the dog's level of understanding.

As you proceed through the following chapters, notice that I invariably give you a gesture or motion to associate with your verbal commands. When saying "no," for instance, I usually point an accusatory finger at the dog. In a multi-pet household, this has the added advantage of letting the errant animal know you mean *him*.

For those times when I am not around to say "no," I am a believer in harmless booby traps, which, again, do communicate with a dog through "body language." For example, one Great Dane had a bad habit of digging soiled linen out of the bathroom clothes hamper. I instructed the owner to get a metal bucket to place on top of the clothes hamper. That way, when the dog lunged for the hamper, the bucket would fall down and scare him.

An equally aggravating habit your dog may have acquired is the acrobatic feat of jumping through the screen door. Once is understandable—a mistake, perhaps. But if he does something once, a continuous pattern is often set for life and might be difficult to break later on. Dogs can't make an intellectual judgment about what or why you do an action. Why shouldn't he continue his flying fun? If you keep replacing the battered screen, the hammer, nails, and rescreening materials all just seem like another one of the endless chores we humans perform each day. He doesn't know that it is a needless repair of his crime, even when you holler. It's not the first time he's heard you yell.

So what do you do about the screen door problem? Simple, if you can catch him in the act. So, set up the situation. To induce him to jump through the door, stand on the side of the door he usually lands on, and get his attention *but without using the command "come."* You must not call him, because he's going to be punished, and if you ever want him to come to you later, he won't. "Come" should be followed only by praise. Excite him, lure him, tempt him, and when he comes near the door, throw a pail of water at him through the screen. This will surprise him and bring him up short. It does wet the floor, but you won't have to replace any more screen doors.

You need not worry that the bucket technique will give your hunting dog an aversion to water, by associating it with punishment. It's the surprise, the sudden wetness, the drastic change in temperature that bothers him, not the water itself. Even Mark Spitz would be put off by an unexpected drenching. Nor should your dog become afraid of buckets, because he'll feel the water before he realizes where it comes from. The first splash will usually cure him of this annoying pastime. If not, the second one will.

Many dogs have a car-chasing problem, and the water bucket works here, too. A New York mailman was plagued by a German short-haired pointer who chased his truck up and down the canyons of the city. I hid inside the mail truck one day and, using my water method, quickly doused the unsuspecting dog. He just as quickly forgot that he had ever met a mail truck.

I don't approve of the traditional methods of discouraging a dog from chasing cars. One school of thought recommends taking along a water pistol to squirt at the dog, but what's a water pistol? The dog will just think it's a game. And filling a water pistol with ammonia is downright dangerous. You could burn his eyes or seriously damage his sense of smell.

The exact procedure I use for stopping car-chasing dogs is simple. Hide in the back of a car with a few buckets of water, and have someone drive the car slowly. When the dog approaches the car and is close enough so that you can't miss, heave the water directly at him, saying "no" as the water hits. Repeat this procedure until the dog stops chasing cars.

A bucket of water is also one way to break your dog of digging holes in the front yard or of rifling the garbage can. The secret is to sneak up on the dog and catch him in the act, so as to preserve the element of surprise. But because your dog can often see you coming, and it does take a while to locate and fill a bucket, it is probably far easier to use your set of house keys. Simply fling them at the errant animal, and when the keys actually connect, tell him "no" loud enough so that he hears you. If you are using this method outdoors, it is a good idea to tie a brightly colored string or ribbon to your keys so they'll be easy to locate after they land.

"No" is the first word your dog should learn. But before you begin obedience training proper, there are a number of other areas of care and control that you and your dog have to cover first.

11 Feeding

In the wild, a dog is a carnivorous predator. But in your home, he has to wait to be fed. How, when, and what he eats are all up to you.

Animals in the wild kill their prey and rip open the stomachs, eating the vital organs—the heart, liver, and lungs—first. This is where the nutrients are, the real food. Pets, however, are dependent on us, and we must remember to feed them a balanced diet.

I will not make blanket statements on anything as vital to an animal as nutrition. It's like a physician saying that all people should avoid cholesterol. But I do believe that, since certain dog-food companies have spent many years perfecting the ideal diet for dogs, it's wise to follow their lead.

As a protest to rising meat prices, two students at the University of Oklahoma recently proved that dog food was very digestible and tastes fine. They even discovered some new applications for dog food in stew and soups, saying that dashes of garlic and salt really bring out the flavor. Their local health director said that there was nothing in dog food to hurt them.

You could slave over the stove preparing the recipes described in the many dog-food cookbooks (oh, yes, they do exist, and for cats, too) and still never achieve the right combination of nutrients and vitamins that a single can of dog food contains. Your pet could die of malnutrition on a diet of prime filet mignon, so if you have any suspicion that your dog is allergic to certan foods, please see your vet. A dog's diet is very important and deserves special attention.

A new puppy being housebroken should eat in the area he's confined in, but at the farthest corner from his toilet, since an animal does not like to relieve himself near where he eats. A dog should eat three times per day until six months old, two times per day up to one year, and then once a day after that.

Always be sure fresh water is available for your dog. He can't ask for it. In one case where a dish was not available, one pair of English setters developed a habit of drinking out of the toilet bowl. I told the owner to make sure the "right" dish was always full, and explained how to break the toilet habit. Use a chopstick or a pencil as a prop to hold up the toilet seat. If a dog goes near it, the lid will fall on his nose.

In another house, I noticed that the Pekinese was showing up with sloppy ears each time he drank from his dish. I told the owners to get him a flat plate, because he couldn't get into a dish with high sides like the one they had.

The woman then asked me how much water to give the dog, and what if he drinks too much? The answer is, he can't. Always leave him a dish of fresh water. He'll learn how much he can handle. One old wives' tale has it that a puppy does not know when to stop drinking and will literally bloat himself if given too much water. That's only partly true. He'll drink until his stomach is full. He won't drink more than is good for him, but unless he's paper trained, he can drink more than is good for *you*.

On the other hand, it is very easy for a dog to *eat* more than is good for him. In the wild, an animal must eat whenever food is available, and so your dog is instinctively programmed never to refuse an offer of food.

Fat owners frequently have fat dogs. One incorrigible Weight Watchers dropout would feed her dog whenever she got the urge to stuff herself. Together they got very chubby and lazy. The dog didn't get nearly enough exercise, since she would wander from restaurant to restaurant with the atrophied dog accompanying her in her roomy purse. Under another owner's care, the dog would eat and exercise properly and probably have a long and happy life.

Your standard dog *always* thinks of food, especially if he smells anything in the least edible, but his intake can be easily controlled by a little discipline on your part. No dog climbs up to the cupboard and opens a can of dog food for himself! Check with your vet to determine how much your dog really needs per day and how often he needs it.

Owners tend to underfeed large dogs and overfeed small ones. A dog will quickly catch on to whatever eating schedule you set up for him. Dogs do not know clock time, certainly, but they catch on to regular schedules such as when you usually return home from work. A dog will anticipate feeding time if he's used to being fed at that time every day. Any dog will adjust if you give him something to adjust to—and this means he should be made to wait till you feed him.

Unless carefully supervised, however, the dominant dog in a multi-dog household will eat the dinner of all the others. And a single animal's ability to put food away at short notice is often astounding. Laraine Day once volunteered her bull mastiff to be a war dog, but he was discharged from the Army because he ate too much. One of my clients reported that a ten-pound beef roast had mysteriously disappeared from the dinner table. After a quick search, they discovered their average-sized hound had devoured the entire cut in a matter of minutes. Since a dog doesn't need to mix saliva with his food as humans do, it doesn't hurt him to bolt his food in enormous gulps. But the sheer quantity he can ingest may well hurt him.

The worst byproduct of canine overeating is called gastric torsion. The exact cause is still a matter of speculation, but the syndrome appears with some regularity in large dogs who have just ingested a big meal and been offered the opportunity to run about. The animal's spleen flips over inside the body, and part or all of the stomach also "capsizes," turning over on itself like an overloaded hammock. The sheer weight of the food acts as a fatal ballast to keep the stomach from righting itself. The esophagus and sometimes the other end of the intestinal tract are twisted, sealing off the stomach as effectively as you would a plastic bag by twisting the open end. The stomach quickly bloats with gas, putting unaccustomed pressure on the dog's vital organs. He soon develops respiratory trouble and goes into shock. Gastric torsion has a high mortality rate, so if your dog's stomach appears bloated, you should recognize this as a potential symptom that requires your veterinarian's immediate attention.

Regular, moderate feeding is only part of your responsibility, however. You'll keep your dog much healthier, and far easier to discipline, if you lay down strict rules that he is *not* allowed to eat except from his dish or from your hand.

It may be a convenience to have your dog vacuum up after you by nosing around under the table for dropped food particles. At least they aren't plentiful enough to cause him any nutritional imbalance, but they do him no good either and merely encourage him to be on the lookout constantly for what's already *on* the table.

When your dog comes to the table and looks up wide-eyed at you, ignore him or send him away. At any rate, pretend it didn't happen. Once you feed a begging dog, he'll return for more food forever and it's your fault. You're the person in charge, so teach him to stay away from the table.

There's something unsettling about a dog mooning at your plate, especially when there's company. But more importantly, as we've seen before, your dog's pitiful begging stare is basically an aggressive action. Once you give in and give him a bite from your plate, your dog will assume you are okaying this act, and the situation can get out of hand very quickly.

One dog was given her regular dog food for dinner, but the family's succulent roast beef tantalized her from the table, so she rejected the standard dog food. Her master offered her another brand and another. Already too much had been made of the whole episode. Finally in desperation, the man gave his dog the roast beef.

It took weeks to get over this small case of giving in. The man adjusted to the dog instead of vice versa, a cardinal sin in training animals. He should have given her one food and left it for twenty minutes, a long enough period of time for the dog to decide if she's going to eat it. If she didn't eat it, he should have taken it away and not offered to feed her again until the next regular feeding time. If it happened again on another night, he should have put the food down for about twenty minutes, then taken it away. Eventually, the dog would have learned that she must eat what and when food is offered to her, not at her own whim.

One woman started by giving her small dog a tidbit from her midnight ham sandwich. Since the meat was more highly flavored than his regular daytime fare, the dog quickly learned to eat only a portion of the food in his dish, to leave room for goodies later on. Since he was eating less and less on his regular dinner, his mistress took to giving him more and more of her sandwich—until he was refusing his dinner altogether and she was feeding him massive doses of ham nightly in the hopes of keeping him alive.

Finally she had to give up her night time snack, eat at the dog's appointed time, and gradually get him back on a dog's schedule.

All of this could have been avoided by simply realizing that she was in control. Once some dogs have accustomed themselves—or more likely, you—to a specific dietary specialty, they may starve themselves for days in the hopes of getting it again, refusing all other food. But realistically the dog is obviously suffering more than you are from his hunger strike, so let him. Eventually, long before either of you suspect it, he'll give in and eat what is offered him. Any premature compassion on your part simply teaches your pet that he can gain rewards through martyrdom, not a pleasant prospect for man or beast.

A dog isn't interested in his own health; he just likes to eat what tastes and smells good. It is your responsibility to make sure he eats properly.

My cookie trick is simply a lesson in control. Quietly and without comment, place a cookie or other morsel on the floor. When your dog goes for it, drop a book beside it and reprimand him with a sharp "no." Repeat the procedure until your dog learns that he cannot touch any loose food until you specifically tell him to. This lesson effectively discourages begging, stealing of loose food, and rifling the groceries or garbage can while your back is turned.

But what kindhearted next-door-type person won't drop your dog a little something if he's whining? As I said before, dogs catch on to schedules, so your dog will learn what time the neighbors go out, too! He'll start hanging around the door when he feels it's time to see them and their pocketfuls of food. Neighbors often encourage other bad habits too. For instance, when you are teaching your dog not to jump up on people, neighbors will often say, "I don't mind him jumping on me. He's so cute." So when you teach your dog not to do something, be sure you alert your friends and neighbors not to encourage it. Everyone wants the dog to be friendly, but such habits as jumping and begging must be stopped with community help.

Discipline plans must also be laid for any dog who has a bad habit of accepting food from just anyone. Have a few people offer him food, then throw a book or your keys at him, telling him "no." He should stop if you do this consistently. Then when you feed him, praise him so he understands the difference. If you want to reward your dog with food, use dog biscuits or dog candy. Scraps only encourage begging and garbage-rifling. Besides, foods prepared for humans aren't necessarily good for dogs, because they aren't always good for us either. If you do want to give your pet scraps from the table, put them in his dish.

Another food-oriented problem is that dogs often dig up plants and devour them. Indoor plants and well-cultivated gardens often come under attack as prime targets. This is because many dog foods don't have any kind of roughage necessary to a dog's diet, and so he must get it somewhere.

Usually the vegetables we eat aren't very tasty to him. He much prefers grass, bark, twigs, and other plants that humans don't use as food. He enjoys them not for their nutritional value alone, but also because dogs strengthen their teeth and gums by chewing heavy roots and plant stems.

There's a legend that if your dog eats grass, it means he's sick. Well, not exactly. It means he will *be* sick, because he's trying to clean out his stomach. Eating grass is usually followed by vomiting. It would be wise to leave your grass-eating dog outside until he's returned the grass to where he found it.

While he's indoors, be sure that all your medicines are safely out of his reach. Many of our pills and capsules come with flavored coating that emits a tantalizing smell, and the contents can wreak havoc in a dog's stomach. My dog once devoured a full envelope of cortisone pills—with no ill effects. Again, recently a news service carried a detailed account of a little Cairn gulping down one hundred thyroid pills with no noticeable effects except a hunger that led him to devour his favorite pillow. These, however, are not usual cases—many times the effects are fatal. Exercise extreme caution where medicines and antidotes are concerned.

If your dog eats a chunk of marijuana or hashish, he will more than likely throw it right up. However, one client's dog ate a mound of hashish and staggered around for three days, but this may be because the owner thought it wise to feed the dog a lot of coffee as an antidote.

I know of another animal that ingested a hallucinogen. The owner picked the dog's front legs up and made him walk around, much as if the creature had taken too many sleeping pills. If your dog eats a depressant, a narcotic, or a poisonous medicine, you should rush him to the vet. But as for small amounts of "soft" drugs, it's best just to let him sleep it off. Remember, though, that drugs, tobacco, liquor have no place in a dog's life unless prescribed by a vet.

In general, the only thing that should go in your dog's stomach is a dog food that says "complete and balanced" on the label. This means it has been tested in the manufacturer's research kennel as a product adequate for the good growth of puppies, and for the maintenance of adult dogs and pregnant and nursing females.

12 Chewing

Jaws and teeth differ from breed to breed, depending somewhat on the trades for which each was bred. The bulldog, bred for bull baiting, has bottom teeth that slant inward and fit very tightly. When he grabs hold, he can hold on forever because his nose is set back and doesn't get in the way.

The greyhound has a very fast and hard chopping bite for bringing down big game on the run. Greyhounds hunt in pairs, are built for speed, but do not have strong-enough jaws to kill anything much bigger than a rabbit. The most perfect set of teeth is on the bull terrier. Besides his teeth, he fights with his head and his legs. The pug's teeth have no aggressive use whatsoever—his jaw is set very much like a bulldog's, but his jaws don't come together and his teeth are spread far apart.

As you are probably aware, man is the only animal who's teeth are so closely set that food particles are easily trapped in between. A dog's teeth are set wider apart, with open spaces of gums in between, so tooth decay from retained food is seldom a problem. As your dog grows older, however, his gums recede slightly from the teeth, leaving spaces where tartar and calculus can accumulate. This site can develop a low-grade abscess, a concentration of bacteria from which your dog's bloodstream will absorb toxins. If these toxins build up, the dog's heart is forced to pump faster so as to filter blood more rapidly through the kidneys, creating a condition technically known as bacterial endocarditis. (The presence of any infection automatically puts extra strain on the kidneys, since the dog must also drink more water so as to flush the toxins from his blood.) The bacteria may be absorbed along with their toxins, and be carried to other sites in the body where they can develop secondary infections including pneumonia, bronchitis, and kidney disease.

All of this can be avoided by using dental floss on your dog's teeth about once a month, getting down below the gum line each time. Be sure, of course, to praise him for his obedience in sitting and staying through this minor ordeal.

If your dog's breath smells, it is probably because his teeth need cleaning or because of the type of food he's eating. Dogs brought up in a nervous household often belch inordinately, and the aroma of digestion lingers on. If your dog seems ravenous or appears to have some other dietary deficiency, the family vet should be consulted.

You must remember, too, that quite apart from hunger, your dog has an instinctive urge to chew. A dog's mouth is his knife, fork, spoon, and fingers all rolled into one. A very little nip at something will tell him whether it's fit to eat or to play with. He knows this as quickly as your fingers tell you. The bite tells him just how hard or heavy an item is.

A dog can control his bite pressure, as a brood bitch when she picks up her baby in her mouth. No hurt occurs there. In fact, it's probably a very secure feeling for the puppy. When your trained hunting dog goes to retrieve the prey, he does not break its skin. He just holds it in his mouth and brings it back.

But dogs are as fond of playing with things with their teeth as we are with our hands. Pups pull each other's tails, bite each other's ears just out of the pleasure of making their teeth meet on something.

Even humans still derive an instinctive pleasure from their teeth. Think of the joy you feel after your teeth have been cleaned by a dentist or when you use dental floss or a toothpick, or even chew on a pencil. "Teething" is apparently a primeval urge ingrained in us all. Your dog is instinctively programmed to chew whatever comes into his mouth, edible or not, so be very careful about what goes in there.

I once found out a dog I was supposed to train had been rushed to the hospital. The animal had chewed up and eaten a plastic pail, and required surgery. Dogs can become violently ill from plastic toys, even from soft rubber ones. Give them only leather chewbones and no rubber toys except a solid hard-rubber ball, not the hollow ones with a bell inside. Not only can they eat these, thereby causing intestinal problems, but they always seem to play with that bell ball when you're fast asleep. Chicken bones can get stuck in his throat. But if you must give him a real bone, give him only boiled soup bones with the end joints sawed off, nothing else.

One unnerved dog owner called me to find out why her dog had such an attraction to a particular spot on their new couch. It seemed the dog would chew only a given eight-inch area, but really went at it with vengeance. A greasy soup bone turned out to be the culprit. The dog had dragged his bone into the living room, tossed it up on the couch, and had a feast. Some of the grease had seeped into the cushions and were sweet reminders to him of treats gone by.

Some dogs go through withdrawal symptoms over a soup bone. Give it to them one time, and they can't get along without it. Allow your dog the luxury of his vice, but let him have it outdoors or cook it so that it's clean.

Once that soup bone soils your couch or rug, your dog will return to the scene of the smell. He'll dig and dig for it, finally chewing a more than noticeable patch in the sofa. He'll even dig into a wooden floor if there is any trace of dripped grease from the soup bone. Serving a bone outside is much more simple than spraying the entire house with a dog repellent.

A dog must have something to chew on because he cleans his teeth that way, but he should be directed in the things he can and can't chew. Replacing bad habits with good ones is only part of the answer. Just because your dog has his grease-free rawhide chew-bone, or thoroughly boiled soup bone that cannot splinter, it doesn't mean he'll leave your own goods alone. When you tell him to hold something in his jaws, he naturally assumes you mean for him to chew it too. He doesn't know that we don't chew our newspapers, shoes, and rugs from time to time. So why shouldn't he?

If a dog is not shown what he *can* have as a chew toy, then he will choose his own, and this can lead to the end of a very pretty living room. The most destructive habit of all is that of the chronic chewer. This habit is set up by you because you let your dog find things to chew on. For example, he starts to chew on an old shoe. He doesn't understand that he is doing something wrong. He adores you, and that shoe smells of you. Besides, leather tastes good.

To correct this shoe chewing, take a minute every day and casually drop your shoe in front of him. Say "no" when he goes for it. If you make the mistake of saying to yourself, "It's all right, I didn't need that shoe, so he can have it as a toy," that opens his thoughts for taking all your shoes. He doesn't know the difference between the old and the new, and he feels you gave him the okay.* Why should he chew on a chew-bone when you've given him a shoe to chew on? You've adjusted to him. Once this happens, he will then start to experiment with all kinds of new taste thrills—wood, paper, plastic, and even your soap pads.

I think the best way to describe a chronic chewer is a dog that really *likes* what he is doing. When your dog chews up the furniture, it's not that he's spitefully trying to get back at you, or show you he was resentful at being left alone. A dog's attention span is too short to make him capable of revenge. He's simply getting involved in the object he's chewing, the way you or I would get involved in a good book.

Vitamin deficiency could be one cause of a dog's chewing things. (It is also a cause of a dog's eating his own stool.) One of my clients switched his dog from a powdered form of a vitamin to the liquid form of the same vitamin, and his three-year-old Dane started chewing papers and magazines. He had not done this since he was a puppy of about four months. After he was switched back to the powdered form of vitamins, it was only a matter of days before he stopped chewing papers and magazines.

I'm not saying that powdered vitamins are always better than liquid, but in this case they were. There are many reasons why a dog will chew, so you have to find out the reason before selecting the technique to solve the problem.

One Airedale landed in deep trouble when his mistress

---

* A dog can ruin your shoes even without chewing on them. When Snap was a small puppy, she used to crawl into one of my boots to go to sleep, and would scratch the leather into shape to make herself more comfortable. She soon dug a hole right through the side.

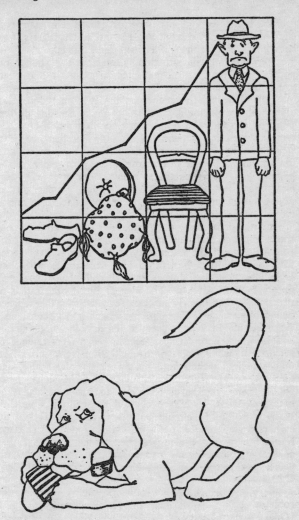

arrived home to find her most treasured Nigerian rug chewed to bits. For whatever reason, great craters had been gouged out of the waffle foam under the rug.

After assaying the situation, I requested a shaker of pepper from the kitchen, made the Airedale sit, and blew some pepper in his nose. Then I took him around with me while I dusted the pepper on the rug, on the corners of tables, and on the sofa. I had to make the dog dislike pepper from the start because it's not that much of a deterrent when simply sprinkled around. For instance, if a steak were flavored with pepper, he'd find the meat taste too appealing. Pepper in his nose makes him really dislike pepper, and then even the smallest traces of it will keep him away. So, seeing the now-detested pepper dusted about was enough to persuade the Airedale to leave things alone.

Another lady had a Weimaraner who chewed her shoes, slippers, and handbags to shreds. She could not afford to support the habit very much longer. My advice was to booby-trap her shoes and accessories with balloons that pop, and stuff them with cellophane or aluminum foil that crackled. (The idea of the booby trap is to surprise—*not* to hurt.) She later reported that this worked beautifully and could she pass the advice on to her friends?

I recommend pepper because it's dry and nonstaining, and harmless booby traps because they're convenient to set up. But what about the true chewing freak? One German shepherd waited until his owner left the house, and then began chewing literally everything in sight: beds, chairs, tables, rugs, even telephone extension cords. If he had been taller, he'd have chewed the ceiling. This time I used a bottle of Tabasco sauce and vinegar. I asked the owner to acquaint his pet with a rag dipped in Tabasco. I told him to put the rag in the dog's mouth, and then apply both vinegar and Tabasco to the various chewing places, taking the dog along on a leash and saying "no" at each stop.

Every day before leaving for work, the owner reminded his dog with a fresh dose of Tabasco, and took him around as he patted the furniture and rugs. But why the vinegar? You'll understand fully in the next chapter on housebreaking, but quite simply, a dog can smell vinegar better than he can Tabasco. The bad taste of Tabasco is a deterrent to chewing per se, but the acid smell of vinegar is associated in a dog's mind with territorial possession. Therefore, the German shepherd was taught that this was his *master's* turf. That acid smell was proof that this was his pack leader's territory. And even when his owner was out, the vinegar smell indicated his owner's territory. But the Tabasco taste was a forceful reminder of what would happen to him if he did overstep his bounds. It worked. After a few days of daily reminders, the shepherd behaved completely. Now this shepherd only chews on the rawhide bone which I told his owner to give him.

When you stop a dog from chewing furniture, shoes, or whatever, you must give him something he is allowed to chew on. You must always replace a bad habit with a good one.

13 Paper Training and Basic Housebreaking

Many cities claim to have eliminated pollution problems. Loggers in the Bull Run Reservoir in Portland, Oregon, use diapers on their horses to protect water quality. The canvas diapers work with snaps, and they're said to be 99 percent effective. The head works engineer, however, pins the major pollution source on deer in the watershed and claims they'd diaper the deer too if they could catch them.

In contrast to horses, deer, and other animals, dogs can be housebroken. But believe it or not, there are those who think that dogs are slightly human in their elimination habits. I was once approached by a group which had spent five thousand dollars inventing a special toilet seat for dogs that would fasten over a standard one.

While cats *can* be taught to use the toilet simply because they have superb balance, a dog cannot. A dog's balance is more evident when he's moving than when he is standing, or sitting still. All but the tiniest dogs will waver and wobble when sitting up. I explained that any toilet seat a dog could use would have to be so heavy and cumbersome that taking it down and setting it up would be more trouble than walking a dog. More than that, however, is the fact that doing what comes naturally to your dog does not mean sitting astride a china commode.

Owners are very concerned about feeding their dogs, but often take little note of eliminating what went in. Both are equally important. Unless you're willing to walk and train a dog, don't buy one—go to F.A.O. Schwarz and get a wind-up toy instead. I tell this to at least three people a day, and I mean it. Puppies are like people. They wet, and like children, they must be trained.

I was once called in when a perfectly housebroken dog apparently slid back into his old habits. This was not impossible, of course, but it seemed unlikely, since I had trained the dog myself—beautifully. I went back to the owner's house, confined the dog, and had him watched around the clock. A little detective work on the maid's day off proved that the culprit was not the dog at all, but the owners' four-year-old boy, who had learned this marvelous exercise from the dog before he was trained. The maid had been cleaning up after him and shielding him from any parental harshness. Clearly a child is under greater social pressure than a dog when it comes to elimination habits, but that's no reason to neglect the dog, who can learn *his* lesson in three weeks flat.

Owners often suggest it's just too much to go through the housebreaking process, and ask me to give the dog to someone else. Obviously, very few people want a dog past the puppy stage who is not in control of his bladder. When I tell them this, it usually serves as a conscience boost to people who are really just going through a lazy phase. The problem must be coped with if your dog is to remain your best friend. I expect the problem to be approached boldly and right now.

I do not believe at all in paper training and find it seriously damaging to the dog's psyche over long periods of time. My major objection to paper training is that a dog should not be taught to do something that is against his nature. It's cruel to both the person and the dog. A dog's urination and defecation are associated with territory and social behavior, and therefore, in our society, with exercise. I recommend paper training only at the start as a temporary method for a puppy until he gets his inoculations against disease, then start housebreaking immediately.

A tiny puppy can contract various diseases, some fatal, if left outside before receiving the proper shots. In this instance, he should be kept inside, and thus paper training is a must. Otherwise, the dog may not be given the chance to grow up.

When people ask me why *paper* training is necessary in the first place, I also explain that immaculate apartments are impossible with a leaky puppy around.

The basics of paper training are simple.

1. *When you bring your puppy home, confine him in a small enclosed area and cover the floor with several layers of newspaper. This will be his home for the next few weeks. Make sure the spot you want him to go on is as far as possible from his food and bed, because dogs don't like to relieve themselves where they sleep and eat. Thus, if you put paper only under his bed and food dish, you're guaranteeing a puddle on the floor.*

2. *Many people feel the puppy will not like the corner they pick out. Not so. Just put him there after feeding, and play with him. He will relieve himself within a few minutes. This sets the pattern for him to follow. Confine the puppy to his enclosed area whenever you are not actually with him, that is, while you're sleeping, working, going out. This will prevent him from relieving himself anywhere else in the house, because the only times your puppy will misbehave is when you're answering the door or telephone or are not at home.*

A young dog quickly learns that he gets reprimanded if he misbehaves in front of you. So the first "lesson" he learns is to become sneaky. You'll have to watch carefully to catch the animal in the act, and the puppy will relieve himself only when your attention is elsewhere. This is why puppies invariably go at the sound of a doorbell or the telephone. It's not nerves, just the assurance that you will be temporarily occupied. The solution is quite simply never to let a puppy out of your sight—or out of his enclosure.

3. *If he gets out of his confined area by mistake or design and does relieve himself in another part of the house—and don't worry, he will!—now you can use his pack instincts to your own advantage. When you come home and see the mess, don't say anything. Ignore your dog. Simply go into the kitchen and get a bottle of Tabasco sauce, a bottle of white vinegar, and a roll of paper towels.*

Uncap the bottles and put them down next to the spot. Then go get your culprit, but without calling him. Bring him, by his collar or by the loose skin at the back of his neck, over to the spot. Keep him right beside you, perhaps holding him firmly between your thighs after you kneel down, until the whole mess is cleaned up. Take a length of paper towel, bunch it up, dip it in the urine or feces, and then put the soiled towels near your dog's nose, telling him "no."

4. Now, you pour a bit of the white vinegar onto the mess on the floor. Then dip another paper towel in it, so that this time it comes away with some of the vinegar. Put the towel in his mouth and again tell him "no." If he won't open his mouth, you can pinch his jowls against his rear teeth.

White vinegar is harmless to dogs and will not stain rugs and furniture, but it does far more than simply disguise the smell. The acid in the vinegar "covers" the smell of the acid in your puppy's urine, in the same way that another dog would if he came by and urinated on the same spot. A dog knows his own urine smell and figures that, unless that odor is covered by another acid smell, he's free to use that spot forever more. You have to show him you're the leader of his pack, but obviously you can't go urinating all over the house to bring it home to him. Rather, you introduce an artificial urine scent that your puppy will quickly recognize as "your" smell. It's very simply a method of establishing *your* territory, without fighting with him or belting him around.

5. When you're all through, put a drop of Tabasco sauce on his gums. This is the actual punishment for his misbehaving. As we've seen earlier, the smells of urine and feces are not disgusting to your dog and are no deterrent in themselves. But your dog's sense of taste is keen enough that the Tabasco sauce on his gums—where just enough will touch his tongue to be unpleasant—will leave a strong mental impression.

If you don't have the time to go through this whole process, you won't have a well-trained dog. He takes a certain amount of training in the beginning, and you have to be willing to give him your time and patience.

Clients usually accept the vinegar-and-Tabasco, paper-

towel method, probably for a number of reasons. It does get the mess cleaned up, and it smacks of magic. Dogs do catch on very fast to it. Be sure to say "no" every time you use the vinegar treatment. He must understand exactly what "no" means.

6. *Once you have reprimanded him, put the puppy back in the papered area. Then sit down and relax. I know how bad you feel about punishing your dog. After you have had a drink and gotten through feeling guilty, go back and play with your puppy in his confined area.*

Just as important as punishment, is reminding him of what he has learned. Two or three times a day, return him to the scene of his crime. Gently touch his nose with a vinegar-soaked paper towel and remind him with a firm "no." Use the Tabasco only when he has actually misbehaved. The vinegar is sufficient threat, a reminder of your presence in the "territory."

You do not have to keep your puppy's room covered with paper forever. After a few days, start to decrease the area covered with papers, and start putting soiled papers in the corner you designate as the temporary toilet area.

With my help, one energetic woman was able, in a few short weeks, to paper train her little black Lhasa apso puppy in a small corner of her apartment. At first she had about six newspapers down and gradually decreased them six inches at a time—an almost unnoticeable reduction to the dog—always putting a circle of vinegar around the paper area. Very soon he was trained to a postage stamp of a paper, and she was delighted. Eventually, you too can use a single length of newspaper, and your dog will be able to hit ground zero with reliable accuracy.

How long should the puppy be confined to his single room? When the papered area decreases to the desired size and the rest of the room remains clean and dry, you can allow him access of the next room, always leaving a way open to the paper. But while you're giving him the freedom of another new room, keep in mind that he might choose to relieve himself when you are distracted. So be prepared. At least for the first few hours, make sure he has your undivided attention. If he goofs, return to the vinegar method.

After the dog has had his inoculations, he should be trained for the streets. For older dogs, paper training is not only unnatural but unfeasible, especially if you are confined to a small city apartment. A dog is not a cat and will not confine himself to a neat plot or area. He will take over the whole place faster than you can mop up behind him. Especially if your dog is going to grow to large proportions, please do remember that paper training is only temporary.

One couple called me for assistance in paper training their St. Bernard puppy. After a preliminary visit, they decided that my fee was a bit out of line and to take care of obedience training and housebreaking by themselves. Two weeks later they called to say that the St. Bernard was, indeed, paper trained. I reminded them that paper training is fine for puppies, and let the incident pass.

But six months later, when their St. Bernard had grown considerably, the couple called again frantically. Their landlord was perturbed at the rotting kitchen floor. The tenants in other apartments couldn't bear the stench. When I arrived, it was worse than I had expected. Not only had the floors warped, but the dog's output had increased so much that it would soak completely through any amount of paper. When the harried owners attempted to pick it up, the paper gave way, leaving the load still on the floor. They were literally cleaning up after him with a snow shovel.

I was immediately hired, of course, even though I now had to charge more to get this older dog, who was set in his ways, detrained from paper. Eventually, both dog and owners got adjusted to going outside, and all was well. This particular case may seem far-fetched, but it is true. You simply must realize that your adult dog needs, for his sake as well as yours, to go outside.

You will notice a male dog, at about six months of age, taking on his characteristic leg-lifting procedure. All puppies, male and female, initially squat to urinate, but because of the angle of the male dog's penis, he can't continue to squat without eventually wetting his own front legs, so he instinctively begins to urinate to one side. Females, by contrast, will continue to squat, and lift their legs only in the rare cases when they want to establish territory.

14 Housebreaking the Older Dog

Once your puppy is perfectly paper trained, all you need do is teach him that the place to go now is outside. Before you *do* take him out, however, you'll do well to complete the basic obedience training steps that are outlined in the next few chapters. He'll be much easier to handle. But whether or not he knows how to sit, stay, and come when called, out he must go—on a leash, if necessary. If you bring along a bundle of his soiled papers, and lay them down in the gutter, it will probably be easier for him to make the connection.

I like to use a very organized method of getting the dogs outside and trained. When you take the dog outside, walk him in a small circle for five or ten minutes, and he should soon relieve himself. If he does it quickly, then take him for a walk as a reward; the exercise will do you both good.

If your dog has difficulty catching on to the outdoors, you can resort to the infallible Loeb Match Method. If after about five minutes he hasn't relieved himself, then insert two or three paper matches, sulfur side out, half-way into your dog's rectum.

Use as many matches as seems necessary—one match will not work inside a Great Dane. It is painless to the dog, but there's only one way for him to remove them, and he will—usually within thirty seconds. By the time the matches come out, everything else does too, and it happens outside, in the right place.

Many owners are concerned about the sulfur going into their dogs' bodies. But the sulfur stays on the outside of the dog, so there is no need for concern. You can use suppositories for the same purpose, but I feel that they take too long to work.

This match method works very well once the owner can bring himself to insert the matches. One not-so-bright client used wooden matches, and a splinter problem developed. I showed another client, who was learning this technique for the first time, how to insert the matches, then I quickly removed them, gave them to her and instructed her to do it herself. She was so intent on doing it just right that she carefully inserted the matches in her mouth to lubricate them, then suddenly realizing what she'd done shot me a guarded look to see if I'd noticed. I looked away, keeping a straight face, and she went ahead and inserted the matches. Today her dog is perfect, but I am sure that if she had seen me laugh, she would have been too flustered to go through with it properly. After a while she realized that the whole thing was just an assist in getting the basic problem handled.

Remember that your dog is a creature of habit and tends to relieve himself in favorite spots. One lady brought her dog along with her to her summer beach house, and was overjoyed when the animal promptly picked out the bathroom for defecation purposes. He wasn't really as intelligent as she claimed. It's just that the bathroom in her city apartment was where she had originally paper-trained him, so of course he picked out the same general place in his new surroundings.

And, naturally enough, this tendency can work against you if your dog has become accustomed to relieving himself indoors. One man had trouble with his beagle, who had learned to relieve himself in the house at a very early age. This was his safe place to go. Now, since puppies remember everything they were taught in the beginning, the dog goes for walks, comes home, and in less than five minutes goes on one special spot in the den. I trained the dog by blocking off the den and teaching the animal not to go in there at all.

I got a phone call from a Detroit family whose Weimaraner had repeatedly soiled the Persian rug and therefore had been confined to the kitchen. Late one night he clawed and chewed a hole through the plasterboard wall to his favorite spot in the living room, defecated there climbed back into the kitchen and went to sleep. I couldn't train him over the phone, but facetiously suggested if the dog was that much a creature of habit, steel walls might help. Later when I was driving through Detroit, I stopped for a few days to handle this problem. The hole in the wall had been left as is. When the owners left for an evening, I stayed behind. As the dog came through the hole in the wall, I heaved two telephone directories at him. He never did it again.

If this general situation seems familiar, you can, again, use your dog's own instincts to your advantage. One of the best ways to correct dogs who have gotten past puppy-hood without being perfectly housebroken is confinement. During the night, restrict him to a very small area—so small that he can't relieve himself without being uncom-fortably close to his own excrement.

During the day, keep the dog close to you, never out of your sight. If this is impossible, put him on an eighteen- to twenty-four-inch long chain (no leather—he can chew through that in seconds) and secure him to something stationary that he can't move, makng sure he can lie down comfortably without choking himself. When you first chain him up, stay with him until he gets used to it, so he won't hurt himself when left alone. Check him periodically to make sure he doesn't get himself all tangled up in his leash.

Be sure the spot you secure him to is *not* his paper-training area. Previously he was praised for going there, so now keep him in a fresh area. Chances are he won't relieve himself, but if he does, reprimand him with vinegar religiously whenever he does.

I don't have too many seemingly hopeless cases, but once I was working with a family to housebreak a diminu-tive dachshund. For some reason I had more trouble with this dog than with any of my other clients, and finally in-structed the family to cage the dog at night and let him out early in the morning. But the dog did not take kindly to being caged and sneaked out of the confinement every evening. No one could figure out how. Late one night, the curious parents decided to hide in an adjacent room. They soon discovered how the dog did it—with a little help from their twelve-year-old son!

Not all owners feel happy about confining their pets, but generally, after a two-to-three-week period, the whole housebreaking problem should be over and done with, *as long as you remember to take the dog out regularly!* And this means at least three or four times a day.

Make sure that he gets outside just before sleep and just after waking, because if you don't automatically think "has the dog been out?" before retiring, there will still be a housebreaking problem. When you wake up in the morning to a puddle, it's probably because you didn't take the dog out, especially if he's been trained for several months. An old, but true, cartoon shows a Scottish terrier watching a clock intently; the caption reads, "If she isn't home by four, I break training."

The advice to make sure the dog gets out may seem self-evident, but people often shirk. At one Fifth Avenue household, the family pet could not be housebroken. I couldn't imagine what the problem was. I retraced my steps in lessons. The maid was to take the dog out four times a day. I had set up a schedule with the family, and everything should have fallen in place. If a trainable dog was failing, obviously there was some physical problem or human failure. I suspected the maid was scamping her duty in walking the dog, and waited in front of the Fifth Avenue building for one entire day. Not once did the maid appear with her charge.

At three years old, a tiny Yorkie was still urinating all over everything. I sat down with the owners and made a schedule of when the dog was to go out. The owners figured they'd get prepared for the cold walk outside each night with a stiff drink. The two are now having five or six refills every night, and the dog never gets out at all. One of my training points is that you learn to control the dog's output. In this case, the owners had to replan *intake*—their own.

Some people shy away from taking their dog out in the rain, teeming or otherwise. Certain dogs love to go outside, no matter what the weather. Others are very reluctant. But the way to get your dog to walk in the rain, and he really must, is to wear a raincoat yourself, and get out there. (Your dog doesn't need one. He has an attractive, carefully lined, all-weather coat. In order for a dog to be housebroken, the dog has to go *somewhere*.

Even the conscientious dogwalker can have problems, however. One dog would relieve himself as soon as his master took his leash off the wall. He knew what the leash meant and figured he'd get it over with. This problem was solved by confining the dog to one area as long as he was inside, as well as having the owner keep the leash hidden in his pocket until they got out.

One ingenious client always had a hard time getting up in the morning to walk his great Pyrenees, so he hired an electrician to rig up an electronic door. The dog could nudge the door by pressing a button and zoom outside. She quickly mastered the exit technique. One spring day when she was in heat,* she made the electronic getaway and returned via the same entry, followed by twenty male dogs. Her owner was awakened by the noise of his many prized belongings being smashed and strewn about the house.

So the motto still holds: If you can't take the dog out, plan to clean up inside. Set up a schedule and follow it, but don't tax the dog's bladder beyond reason. See that he gets out at least three or four times per day, or take him out automatically after *you* go yourself.

Some owners insist on using toilet paper on their dogs' behinds. One lady I know uses flip-tops from Coca-Cola cans to clean any excess that may stick to her dog's hair. Certain dogs seem to require it for the sake of appearance, as they have long hair that doesn't look good when soiled. Obviously they have to be cleaned with something. If not, they may rub themselves clean on the furniture. I don't suggest shaving them—dogs' shaved behinds look like targets—but some people do it anyway.

Housebreaking is not as difficult as it seems, especially when you stop trying to reason with the animal as though he were a child. Make it as simple as possible for yourself by leaving as little room as possible for the dog to make a mistake.

But what if he *does* break training?

---

* Mating cycle for female dogs.

15 What If He Breaks Training?

Aside from the will power/discipline factor, which only the owner can provide, some dogs really *are* difficult to train. Some have double bladders, as did one that I handled, and only one bladder can relieve itself at a time. But all too many people feel they have "paid their dues" during the initial housebreaking and hope against hope that the problem will remain solved.

One client bragged to me on how well her pet was housebroken. I listened patiently, suspecting that the lady was exaggerating a bit. And indeed, one New Year's Eve, ten seconds before midnight, amidst a house full of holiday company, this dog who never messed in the house, made a dramatic New Year's resolution. His owner finally broke down and said that *sometimes* her dog had an accident and would I please assist? That was no accident, that was her dog.

Another client whose dog I was training regularly found damp spots on his couch but swore his dog couldn't do such a thing as urinate on the furniture. He was convinced that it was moisture in the air. I had him put down a plastic covering. Miraculously, a yellow puddle appeared from nowhere.

Lots of well-meaning people would rather clean up the mess than listen to the harangue that comes down on the dog if caught, so the dogs just continue. Everyone involved in training the dog has to feel responsible. Every time the dog messes, he has to be reprimanded. If your best friend came in and peed on your rug, you'd certainly say something—so give your dog the same respect. If it's still happening, it's because you're letting it happen.

Even the best-trained dog will break training under special circumstances, such as when his territorial rights are threatened. When a strange dog comes into your house and urinates on a corner of your stairs, you are so horrified that you might not notice your own dog doing the same thing on the same spot. One woman imported a female in heat for her perfectly housebroken male dog to mate with, and afterward, he lifted his leg throughout the apartment. He was simply reestablishing his territory in case the bitch ever returned. This is a natural and inevitable post-coital response, and I pointed out that the obvious answer was never to allow dogs to mate in the males' domain—take *him* to *her*.

Months of housebreaking may still fail if your dog is on a high-protein diet. Too much meat—and also eggs, cheese, toast, and butter—produce more uric acid, and a corresponding need to urinate much more frequently.

If your aging dog has sudden or even occasional housebreaking problems, check with your vet promptly. Never wait for such a problem to subside. Your dog may be ill.

If your dog breaks training once in a great while, it's no real cause for worry. Possibly he's sick, and just couldn't wait to get outside. If so, you should be able to detect some change in his other habits and behavior. *But in any case, reprimand him as if he had planned to do it!*

If he feels that there are any exceptions to the rule, he'll soon find some other excuse to do as he pleases. Once you let your dog get away with soiling the house after he has been trained not to, you'll need twice the effort to get him back in line.

One of my clients called me one evening to report that it had been raining for days and she strongly disliked taking the dog out in the wet. So, of course, he went on the rug. "How could I punish him when it was my fault?" I explained that she would *have* to punish the dog, or they would have to start the process all over again. She did not follow my directions. The next sunny day, the dog went again on the same exact spot. "It wasn't my fault," she said. "I took him out." This is an example of how each day really does count in training your dog. Cleaning up without correcting him gives the dog the go-ahead to do it again. If you aren't consistent with your dogs, how else will they know when you're serious?

I once visited two poodles who were never really sure

that their masters didn't want them to go in the house. Sometimes it seemed all right to them, and other times, when the masters were in foul moods, it was disastrous. As a result, the dogs had reached the ages of five and seven without permanent training, and were tied to the bedroom door each night with paper all around. You should look at your dog's every act as an embryonic habit, and act accordingly.

In the struggle to train your dog, always remember that he will forever test you to see if this silly business about relieving himself only out-of-doors is for real. Long after you've gotten him officially trained, he will continue to test you, so be alert. Remember that a dog uses his leg-lifting as one means of testing to see who's in charge. Whenever one dog did a trick properly, he lifted his leg. This is an aggressive act and one that should be curbed immediately, for that reason alone.

At one point, Inches, my Maltese, was not defecating along with all the other dogs when they went out for their daily runs. We couldn't figure out where he was doing it, because there was no smell. Then one day, I was adjusting the stereo and stooped to look behind it. Inches had been crawling back there, and the reason we didn't smell anything was because the air conditioning was pulling the odor right outside, and the moving air had dried out all his stool.

So to break Inches of this habit, I waited up one night in another corner of the living room. About 1:00 A.M., sure enough, Inches came padding in. As soon as he started to crawl behind the stereo, I threw one of my boots at him. It hit the stereo instead of him. I had to pay a hundred dollars to fix the stereo, but the noise cured him of going back there—or anywhere else indoors, for that matter.

At another household the excrement problem was doubly bad because two dogs were doing the dirty work. I had to confine one to find out which was the culprit. (Catching dogs in the act is very important in solving the problem, although it can be solved by confinement alone.)

If your dog regresses, use the vinegar method when you clean it up. Make such a procedure out of it that the dog will never think of doing it again. In fact, the threat of going through the whole catastrophe another time should keep *you* motivated.

All mistakes *must* be handled by the *vinegar and paper method* mentioned before. Take him to the soiled area, and correct him with vinegar. If he continuously makes mistakes, then confine him to the spot where he was originally confined for housebreaking. He must learn that he can have the run of the house only if he doesn't relieve himself there.

If his misbehavior has become well established, however, the vinegar method won't work overnight. You have to chip away at the habit bit by bit, which was the way he built it up.

If you're not positive that your dog has his instructions down pat, remind him each day, but not with words alone. *Show* him. Before leaving the house in the morning, take your dog to the area where he has previously made mistakes. Using a paper towel, pat a dab of vinegar on the places he's misbehaved. Then touch the vinegar to his nose, telling him "no." The vinegar smell should remind him all day. Eventually your command alone will be sufficient, but the more you combine actions with words, the quicker he'll learn and the longer he'll remember. If all this is done religiously sooner or later he'll learn to control his toilet habits. You'll soon be able to forget bending, stooping, and mopping up, and come to enjoy your dog even more.

Remember, be consistent. Always finish what you start, and never lose your temper.

Your dog's stool should be collected and taken to your veterinarian about every six months. At the same time take your dog in for his checkup. Do this with the same regularity that you go to your doctor for a physical examination.

One day while I was bending over in the gutter to get my dog's stool sample for the vet, a burly truckdriver loomed up, and commented, "Some people collect the strangest things." Forget about public opinion. If you can't bring the stool sample in, you may be withholding vital information from your vet. The only way to detect worms, blood, and a million other digestive problems is by examining your dog's stool under a microscope.

Remember, though—when you collect your sample, try not to scoop up too much of the surrounding environment. A friend of mine was convinced his dog had worms, and brought me a sample of his dog's stool to prove it. When I opened the plastic envelope, out slid a caterpillar. "I was right," the man said gravely. "He *does* have worms after all."

16 Whining, Barking, and Jumping

Just as push often leads to shove, growling often leads to biting. The dog knows perfectly well that his bark is an embryonic bite, and he has to realize you do too. Otherwise, he will simply take it that you are not challenging his bid for supremacy, and quite obediently, he will progress to the next level of obnoxiousness.

Initially, a puppy whines because he feels that he's very small and alone—it's like a baby's cry. Your puppy will whine when he's unhappy but, just like a baby, *also when he wants something*. Remember when you first got your dog? You cuddled him and kissed him? Then you put him to bed in another room. First he whined to get your attention, and then, when you didn't come to him, he started to bark and cry louder and louder. You probably thought you were being cruel to him because you locked him up all by himself, so you went in to soothe him. Therefore, he discovered that you would come and comfort him if he whined—and the habit was off and running.

Whining should be curtailed immediately. Otherwise, it may well grow up to be barking. If you let this habit go, soon you'll have a full-fidelity barker. He'll bark automatically when he grows larger and feels more self-confident, because he has learned he can get attention or whatever comes from barking.

Unless a dog is reprimanded for his noisemaking, he may grow into an obnoxious animal. "He's not aggressive," the owners often tell me. "He just has a tendency to bark at people." But what at first might seem like a harmless, friendly bark can, through the unintentional praise of the master, turn a dog into a spoiled brat.

How does one avert this behavioral equivalent of the Domino Theory? Naturally, the place aggression should be nipped is in the bud, which in your dog's case could be whining.

Even an older dog will whine with excitement when he suspects he's going to be offered a run in the park or a special tidbit. It's the rough equivalent of a pleased giggle, but at the same time it is a pleading noise, a means of making you feel sorry for him, a manipulative gesture. When your dog, puppy or adult, starts to whine, see if he's in trouble. If everything's all right—no stones caught between his pads, no cuts on the inside of his leg where it's less noticeable, no female dog mooning at him through the window—then discourage the noise immediately!

Even if your dog's request seems to be reasonable, such as when he's whining in anticipation of going out, stop him with a firm "no." When you've been away from home and your dog hasn't seen you in some time, he'll frequently whine with sheer excitement. In this case, accept your greeting without letting him jump up on you, then calm him down.

If he whines to get out of the car when he sees another dog, tell him "no." If he persists in whining, reprimand him firmly, repeating your "no." Make it clear that you don't want him to whine. Dogs are very much like children in this respect. If you tell them "no" in no uncertain terms, they will listen. But if you ignore their bad behavior, they will become obstreperous.

Barking is more annoying simply because it's louder. Some people find the basenji perfect because it doesn't bark, but all other dogs do bark and love it. If for any reason you *want* your dog to bark, you'll find full instructions on inciting and controlling barking in the chapter "Defense Pets." But because a dog will almost invariably bark on his own, it's better to start by teaching him when he's *not* supposed to.

Generally a dog will react, or overreact, to anything he feels is different from the norm. Most dogs bark when they notice a strange noise, especially when you're away, and they have no clue as to how they ought to behave. When the "pack leader" is away, it's up to the remaining dog to defend the territory against intruders.

One mixed breed who had been born in the winter, and who had inherited his Labrador father's eyesight, barked at his master one June day when he saw him downwind without his shirt on. When his owner came into the dog's range of sight and smell, the dog went into a paroxysm of "embarrassed" submission, for having mistaken his identity.

A young puppy associates the elevator with his master's comings and goings, so the sound excites him even if his master is settled down reading the paper. Older dogs are less likely to bark unnecessarily, simply because they've learned that elevator noises don't mean anything unless they are followed by footsteps outside the door.

To a puppy, however, *everything* is new and exciting, and so he will bark at everything. But just because he'll eventually calm down is no reason to let him keep on barking, because "eventually" could be years.

Some excitable dogs will work themselves into hysterical fits of barking, even when the owner tells them to stop. They have become so worked up that the barks keep on coming, like hiccups. Or the dog may decide to erupt in barking at 4:00 A.M.

Many predatory animals do their hunting at night, and so nighttime will put dogs instinctively on the alert. Unexpected noises and movements that wouldn't faze him during the day may elicit a warning growl.

Now is the time to praise or discourage him, depending on whether you want him to be on guard or utterly phlegmatic. (But don't make *too* big a thing out of unexpected night noises, or he may carry over his excitability into the daytime as well.) You may as well get your dog used to things he is going to have to live with. Train him to accept loud noises, strange movements, and unusual situations. Bring possible problems out in the open —deliberately set up situations and show him there's no reason for fright. Calm him down by patting him and talking to him in a soothing voice.

One sleepless owner listened while I explained the various antibarking techniques. "Do you expect me to go to all that trouble at 4:00 A.M.?" he then asked. "Besides, the dog's incorrigible."

Actually, he was, for not getting up. A dog wants to know what he can and cannot do. He needs to know authority. If you want him to stop barking, you have to do something to bring it about, *now*.

Humans tend to figure out too many ways not to do things right. One secretary taped her dog's mouth shut to soothe the nervous neighbor's nerves. "It doesn't hurt him," she claimed. "I used the tape with air holes in it!" She must have assumed it wouldn't pull his hair. Fortunately, she kept the dog for only fourteen weeks.

One mechanical device that does stop barking—automatically—is an electronic collar fitted with a microphone. The sound of the dog's own bark triggers the collar to deliver a harmless but unpleasant electric shock. This device comes in sizes to suit your dog.

But your dog should learn to obey you, not a set of external circumstances he can't understand. A shock collar can teach him only one thing. You can train him much more thoroughly, simply by being there and relating to him.

If you want your dog to stop barking without devices, which is the way you should do it, gently hold his muzzle when he starts barking. Say "no." Then praise him when he stops. If the elevator's movement makes your dog bark, then use the same technique. When you hear it coming, put your hand over his muzzle and say "no." Very simple but very effective.

Remember not to praise your dog before he's been corrected. This is of the utmost importance. Most dogs that have attacked people have in some way been taught to be aggressive. I don't mean only attack-trained dogs. I mean all dogs that are praised for committing aggressive acts. Many owners who want their dogs to be aggressive say "good boy" when their dogs bark or growl at anybody. But many people who *don't* want their dogs to bark or be aggressive say, "Be a good boy and don't do that." Without realizing it, they are in fact praising their dog for being aggressive.

You must be utterly calm while training your dog about barking, showing him, by example, that there's nothing to get excited about. Otherwise, the two of you will probably both give up in despair. If you go through the motions carefully, it will come in time. A firm "no" whenever he barks at the wrong time should bring about the proper response. Of course some dogs need an added incentive to stop barking.

For example, a collie who was brand new to his family, and very alert to everything they did and said, had one major drawback. He barked every time visitors came to the door, which startled them. His mistress was squeamish about disciplining his barking, but finally, after her friends refused to visit, she decided it had to be stopped.

I simply instructed her to drop the Yellow Pages near the barking dog. A phone book makes a startling thud, and pretty soon the collie got the point and stopped barking. In fact, whenever a dog growls or barks, any magazine tossed in his direction will usually stop him.

What do you do if your dog barks only when you're not thinking about training? First of all, you should *always* be thinking about training, or you'll never get the dog trained.

Many dogs misbehave only when their masters are gone. Certainly you know—or more likely, have heard—dogs who whine or bark around the house all day once their master has gone to work. Perhaps the owner doesn't know this. If so it really is your duty to tell him—in a nice way, so he doesn't start growling on his own. How can he correct something he doesn't know exists?

If you suspect *your* dog barks only when you're out of the house, ask your neighbors. If he does, chances are they'll be only too glad to tell you. But do make sure it's your own pet who's really at fault. One lady on Fire Island kept getting complaining calls from her neighbors that her dog's barking and howling had to stop. She would stay up nights trying to figure out why they thought her silent dog was such a nuisance. Then she did a little skulking about and found that the barking was coming from another house. The local acoustics were somewhat odd and capable of playing tricks on the ears. After much apology, the neighborhood got back to normal, and the true barker was singled out.

Patience is the most helpful factor in training and in correcting a dog who barks when he's alone. Plan to spend some time on the problem. Take your dog for a walk in the park, then take him home. Hide outside to find out if he barks when you leave. If he does, take him out again, and while you are out, have someone else hide inside the house. Leave the radio on to disguise any noises, and use an electric fan, blowing in your friend's direction, to keep him from being sniffed out.

Bring your dog back, then tell him good-bye and leave. If he goes into his act of barking, the hidden individual should throw a book or magazine in his direction and shout "no." The whole point of this exercise is to keep your dog uncertain about whether or not you're actually at home. Repeat it once a day until he remains silent.

If your dog is cured of barking but leaps at the door, one of the best things you can do is to buy a box of balloons. You can get about fifty or so in a package for a dollar. Sit down on the floor and start blowing the balloons full of air. When your dog comes over to see what you are doing, burst one balloon in his face. It won't hurt him, but it certainly will startle him, which is what you want to do. Repeat this with another balloon and another until the dog is scared by the loud bangs and simply goes away from the area.

While you're doing this to him, don't say anything. Some people call their dog to them and then do it. If you do this, your dog will probably never come to you when you do want him. Just keep your mouth shut.

Your dog won't go near the balloons now, because he feels they might explode if he does. So take the balloons and put them on the door he jumps on. Tape them right on the door, at the level his jaws and muzzle reach. Since he has been shying away from the balloons, he will probably stay away from the door too. After a week or so, take the balloons down, and your dog should be cured. (Incidentally, once your dog is shy of balloons, you can also use them to keep him out of the garbage can by tucking one under the lid.) The only drawback to this technique is that when friends drop in to visit and see the balloons they will ask why they weren't invited to the party.

Some dogs want to jump up on everyone they see. I once noticed a young lady being plagued by her dog jumping up on her in the street. I offered to help her teach the dog to stop. "No," she said, "I kind of like it." Later the dog jumped up and broke her teeth, and she finally understood my offer.

This particularly annoying habit *can* be stopped quickly. If it's a small dog who's the jumper, wait until he jumps, then grab the elbows of his front legs and lift him up toward you. His hindquarters will swing in between your legs, and you can set him down gently on his back, at the same time saying "no." Dogs don't like this position, because it upsets their sense of balance, and so they will quickly learn not to jump if it means being flipped over.

A larger dog should be given a hard knee to the chest —a real jolt. I say hard because an owner will automatically pull his punch and not hurt the dog, but he has to do it with *some* force or it just won't work. Another method is simply to step gently on his hind paws. He will automatically back away to keep from being stepped on.

Anyone he jumps on should be told to knee the dog or push him away. Remember to say "no" when you do it. Dogs are very much creatures of habit, and bowling the dog over every time he jumps up will make him stop after only a few tries. One feisty Bouvier, despite being flipped, could not walk down the street without lunging out at people. I fixed this problem by walking down the street myself one night. When I came face to face with the dog and the dog lunged, I swung my jacket at him, saying "no." Shocked, the dog stopped. The owner repeated this with a different friend each evening, and the dog quickly fell in line. After a while, your dog will learn the difference between playing with you and jumping on you.

17 Biting

One of my major tenets in dog training is that there is no such thing as a friendly nip. But convincing dog owners of this is sometimes a headache.

Dogs learn to bite at an early age. Small puppies nip playfully at your hand while you are playing with them. They have been used to biting at their brothers and sisters in the litter, and to them you are just a substitute.

The way to stop this is to put one hand in the puppy's mouth. With the other, continually tap him on the side of his snoot, using the word "no." When he lets go and backs away from your hand, praise him. Puppies *must* be shown immediately that nipping is not wanted, because puppy nipping can become a biting habit.

Remember that your dog does not *have* to become a barker before he starts biting. Even if he has been trained not to bark, he may still bite. One family had a problem with their dog nipping the children. The kids had it coming, because they teased the dog, and you would expect something on the order of a small bite to occur. My advice to these parents was to set up possible nipping situations with the dog and the children. I instructed them to keep a magazine or rolled newspaper tucked under their arms as often as possible, to be tossed at the dog whenever he attempted to nip. If the paper were held in the hand, rather than under the arm, the dog would see it and anticipate what was coming, thus destroying our main weapon, the element of surprise. I told the parents to tell the children to "go and play," but not tease, and then toss the magazine at the dog if he went for them. I reminded them not to scream at the children or the dog, but just to toss the magazine methodically and say "no" when it hit.

Bear in mind that what you might think is punishment could be play to your dog, especially if you have spent a lot of time letting him snap and pick at you playfully. When the dog is older and understands, then you won't have to carry the rolled paper around anymore. Right now, he'll obey you because he can't tell when you have the paper. But it's best to teach the dog manners while he is young, rather than wait until he's set in his ways.

You've got to be vigilant in the beginning because the older a dog gets, the more he learns that he will get his own way by biting, and the habit is harder to stop.

All dogs can bite awfully hard. A shepherd has a bite of about eight hundred pounds per square inch, a Doberman one of about seven hundred. Even little dogs can bite a lot harder than any human. So think about it, it's you who will get hurt. When dogs grow older and are still biting, all too many owners give in to them out of fear. In one family, the dog and master were in competition for control of the family. The dog won, because he had bigger teeth. Another dog owner, a very sweet, retiring man, was scared of his biting dog but didn't like to admit it. I asked him how long his dog had been biting. "Five years," he replied.

I told him the only way I could break his dog overnight was to take his teeth out. Not because I couldn't stop the dog from biting, but because the man was really frightened of his dog and unless he got over this fear nothing could be done.

The same type of situation occurred with a Lhasa apso who quickly found out his mistress was frightened of him and began biting her, but no one else. I felt she could *never* control her dog, and it was senseless even to try training. So I suggested she give him to someone who understood animals and was not frightened of them.

The woman was incensed, of course, so she got another trainer. His training was effective for a short time, but then the dog went back to his same old aggressive habits, because he discovered the trainer was only temporary and the woman's attitude hadn't changed.

I have been bitten only once in my fifteen years of training, and the story is worth repeating if only to emphasize that a dog's size means nothing when it comes to biting. A family that had never owned a dog before and wanted a guard dog invested a thousand dollars in the purchase and training of a fifteen-pound dog. By the time he was two years old, the dog had bitten sixteen people and was registered under five different names in the city license bureau, since New York law provides that a dog must be put to sleep if it bites more than twice. When these people called me, I insisted on a few safeguards, and told them to have their dog either on a leash, in a muzzle, or in another room with the door closed.

When I made my preliminary visit, I brought my daughter Stephanie and my own dog along. We all settled down, and the lady of the house began discussing the family's problems. At this point, the woman's daughter began feeling sorry for her dog, who had been confined to another room, and went to solace him for being left alone. I was relaxing in a chair, with my arms hanging loosely over the sides. Suddenly the dog came barreling through the opened door, attached himself to my hand, and literally hung there. I finally managed to shake the dog off, and Plum immediately pinned him. The daughter of the household rescued her pet, and with the dog in her arms, raced crying from the room, her mother after her. The maid rushed in to mop up the blood-stained carpet. And I stood there bleeding. . . . . . . My hand required sixteen stitches when I reached the emergency room of the local hospital—two hours later. (The dog, incidentally, was put away—but not on my account.)

There are times when a dog will bite out of reflex. For instance, when he's in a fight, terrified or in real distress. One dog tore his mistress's hand to shreds, and she supposed he was getting even because her estranged husband had kicked the dog on his last visit. As it turned out, the husband's kick had dislocated a disk in the dog's spine, and he was in acute pain.

Any dog you suspect has been injured should be muzzled as a precaution. But in normal circumstances, the dog must be reprimanded for biting, or *any* kind of aggressive act. Another client of mine had her lip badly torn by her dog, twenty-six stitches worth. She told me that she blamed herself for the accident, however, because she had taken her dog's food away before he had finished it. When he bites again, no matter what the circumstances, she'll probably find another way to blame herself. This is the most common mistake made when coping with a biting dog. A firm reprimand at the first sign of aggression, *playful or otherwise,* is the answer, not the excuses. Whatever he does wrong, correct him immediately, right there on the spot.

In Chapter 7, we discussed the man whose dog bit him on the hand. I advised him to reprimand his dog firmly, to establish that this behavior was plainly unacceptable. This is what you *must* do with a biter—exert the sheer force that you were too reluctant to administer earlier, when it was necessary. Then consider the incident over and hold no grudge.

In another situation, a four-pound poodle had been allowed to take over the whole house. The dog had every room sewed up for his very own. He growled and bit, while people cowered about the house. I taught this particular family not to be afraid, but simply to hold out one hand when the poodle charged. The dog quickly learned never to bite a hand, only to lick it affectionately, because if he behaved otherwise, he got whacked soundly.

For the chronic biter I am forced to employ more dramatic methods. One day my answering machine recorded a call from a family whose dachshund had literally cornered most of them in the bathroom. I didn't wait for the rest of the message. I rushed out the door, into my car, careened across town, double parked, and raced up the stairs to a third-floor apartment. A little boy let me in, and I grabbed one of the coats out of the entrance-hall closet on my way past. This coat was what I used to throw over the dachshund, most of whose family was indeed corralled in the bathroom.

It had happened before, many times, and they would never listen to my advice, but I was very firm with them this time. I laid down strict laws on how to handle the situation. I told them to offer a sleeve or a stick. When the dog bit it, they were to cover his head with a coat or blanket. No animal likes having his head covered, and this not only keeps the animal from biting, but reinforces the point that you are more "powerful" and immune to being bitten. But be very careful to cover the dog's head *completely,* or have a good doctor handy.

I warned them that if the dog ever cornered them in the bathroom again, I'd let them all rot in there! When I got downstairs, I found my double-parked car had been towed away by the police.

18 Why Dogs Fight and Kill

No one wants a dog who bites *people,* but certain dog owners are drawn toward the idea of a pet who can take on the neighborhood dogs. One such family told me that they needed a "family dog." One that doesn't soil the house, doesn't bark, is friendly to guests, doesn't have a ravenous appetite. I suggested a poodle. "No," they said, "that breed of dog is too meek, he couldn't stand up to a shepherd. And he couldn't beat a pit bull or Doberman." What they were really interested in was a killer, so I told them to get a lion.

I was walking Plum one evening in the park when we came in sight of a man about 5 feet 2 inchs leading a mammoth Great Dane. "Watch out," the man shouted. "I can't control my dog."

Despite his warning, I was a bit surprised when the Dane went for Plum. Plum held off the Dane, but when the whole episode repeated itself on a second evening, I had to break up the fight. This time I let the man know he had no business owning, let alone walking, a dog he couldn't or wouldn't control.

During daylight, however, this same Dane cornered Plum a third time and got a grip on his neck. Plum got away, but not without a savage gash that narrowly missed his jugular vein. I knew that Plum had been very badly hurt because of the smell of death about him. It's simply an odor of deathly fear. I feel this dog owner was secretly enjoying the way his Dane handled himself. It's dog owners like this who need watching, not their dogs, who are only behaving in a way that they feel their masters approve.

A lady wheeling twins once jibed at me because Plum didn't try to attack her poodles. "He didn't even growl at them. He's not much of a man." I jokingly told her to watch out or I would have him bite their heads off. Probably this lady chastises her bitch for aggressive behavior, but encourages her male poodle to assert his masculinity.

One family loved to see their dog fight with other dogs so much that they had their living room penned off with chicken wire, so that the battling dogs didn't ruin the furniture. They didn't want the animal corrected; that would break his spirit, they said.

More often than not, such owners are using their dogs to express their own repressed aggressions. All I have to say to those who feel it is all right to let dogs fight and "work out their own problems" is that allowing or encouraging bloodshed is cruel and unnecessary. Strikes are resolved by arbitration, not by pitched battles of scabs and pickets. Why deny your dog the benefits of your own common sense?

As a dog owner, it's your duty to see that your animal behaves. A master should be able to resolve *any* dog's problems with a single "no." Unfortunately an owner trying to calm his dog often uses the words "good boy," thus unintentionally reinforcing his dog's tendency to go after other dogs. The word to use is "no"—and if you're out walking, jerk the lead firmly to make sure the dog understands that he is not to act this way.

To keep your dog nonviolent when another dog visits, make sure that all of your dog's food, water, and toys of any kind are not lying around. The newcomer is bound to show an interest in them, and your dog will want to protect his own turf. Putting the stuff away doesn't necessarily mean there won't be a fight, but it does minimize the possibility.

There are various ways of stopping a fight if you are too late to prevent it. The cardinal rule is to focus on your own dog but only if the other dog's owner is focusing on his. Any dog is more likely to obey his own master's commands, but if you try to hold your dog while there's no one to hold the other dog, your pet will get the worst of it.

Rule Number Two is to keep yourself at one end or

the other, not in the middle where the biting is going on. With a small ten-pound dog, it's easy. Just pick him up bodily and tell him "no." If the dog is too hefty to lift, grab him by the tail or hind legs and pull. If the other dog's owner isn't following your example, then grab his dog and at the same time yell "no" to your dog. You can control yours by voice, but not his.

Often in a fight, one dog gets a grip on the other and won't let go, even if his hindquarters have left the ground. As long as the mouth is closed, you're relatively safe. Simply insert a stout stick behind the dog's canine teeth (he has to hold his mouth fairly wide open to get a grip to begin with) and force his jaws apart. If you can, cover his nose with your free hand so that he has to breathe through his mouth and thus must release his grip. A fighting dog is breathing heavily, and simply cannot hold his breath more than a few seconds.

Once the dogs are separated, move out fast. Since most dogfights are over territory, simply removing your dog from the scene of battle—or even a few feet away —should cool things off.

If your dog has a habit of killing small birds and animals, you can stop it quickly. The next time he kills something, immediately tie the dead carcass tightly around his neck, where he can't reach it with his jaws, and then confine him to a small area. He will try to paw the carcass loose. When he tries, reprimand him sharply, tell him "no," and give him a firm slap, if necessary.

Then set him free, but leave the carcass on him for a few days. The sight may be unpleasant for you, but the sensation will be even worse for him. This may seem cruel, but he will no longer be knocking off the local wildlife. Although this procedure may seem reminiscent of the Ancient Mariner, who had an albatross he had wantonly killed hung around his neck, it is actually an old farmer's trick to keep dogs from molesting chickens.

19 Adapting Your Dog to a Human Environment

One day I took my four dogs to a friend's country house. But since his last visit, I had added a third Maltese, Snap, to my private pack. When I let them out of the car, all four dogs bounded down toward the swimming pool area. Plum, Inches, and Sleepy had been there before and moreover knew what a swimming pool was, so they stopped short at the tiled perimeter. But Snap, who hadn't seen a swimming pool before, kept right on going.

A dog can learn that he's fed at four o'clock, or that you will be unhappy if he chews your tennis racket, but he is simply unable to use what we call logic and come to his own conclusions about something he hasn't experienced. This is why dogs are so insatiably curious. They *have* to smell, taste, chew, or nudge things to be able to understand them.

In the wild, your dog would rely on his instinct for survival, but in the home, where he is now faced with manmade objects, *you* have to teach him how to survive, and the only way to do this is to train him.

You certainly consider your living room a fairly safe place, and yet to a small child, it would be a wilderness of truly awesome hazards. A glass vase can shatter into vicious shards. An electric extension cord can deliver an excruciating shock. A heavy paperweight can fall, causing a concussion. Your dog is prone to the same hazards, only more so, for he has far more strength and agility to knock things over with, plus a highly efficient set of teeth that enable him to get through hard protective surfaces, down

121

to the real danger inside. You simply must do his thinking for him, or more accurately, his anticipating.

I came right out and told one client that he was an imbecile for letting his dog run loose in the house while he was trying to paint the kitchen floor—the animal didn't know what the "wet paint" sign meant. Sure enough, the dog soon trucked on over to his water dish in the corner, leaving a charming footprint pattern. Take this as a lesson if you plan any redecorating. Somehow, your dog will find a way to climb your wall if it's the one that you're painting.

When Christmas comes around, pay particular attention to the way you decorate your home. Dangling metal tinsel can kill your dog. It often contains lead, which can poison him, and if he leaps for it, he can topple the whole tree. Be very careful with candles on trees. A dog can make a mistake and knock the tree down, but he can't open the door and run out when a fire starts.

Make sure that you know where the potential danger lies. Small dogs are subject to special dangers simply because of their size. A falling book or a thrown shoe can give a Pekinese a concussion, and maybe worse.

Never let your dog get away with any bad habits which could eventually become harmful to him. No matter how bad you feel, you *must* reprimand him. Oftentimes people's guilt feelings prevent them from doing something which, in the final analysis, is the best thing for their dog.

If he steps off the curb, jerk him back as hard as you can and tell him "no." When he is back on the curb, praise him, then step off yourself, giving his leash another jerk to have him follow. Let him know in no uncertain terms that the only time he can step off the curb is after you have done so yourself. This should help to insure your dog a long life.

Keep your pet from playing with plastic containers, eating poisonous substances and pills, chasing cars, and all the other activities that could hurt him. Your common sense should tell you what they are. For instance, I specifically warn people to train their dogs not to chew electric wires. To do this, take a bottle of Tabasco sauce, let him taste it undiluted, and then coat the wires with it.

The same thing holds true for any other dangerous objects. In fact don't even wait for situations to occur but set them up. Put the electric fan on the floor, and let the dog see you playing with it. His curiosity will bring him over to it. Never call him. When he does start sniffing at the fan, give him a good whack and tell him "no." You might think that this is a bit harsh because you actually enticed him to do it, but just think of what the blades can do to him if he went to play with the fan any other time.

Other potential canine hazards are not so obvious, however. For instance, when you go bicycle riding and take your dog along for the exercise, you may be doing him more harm than good. If your dog is running free beside you, he can adapt his own gait to move at a rhythm he finds comfortable. But if he's attached to your bike by a leash, this means that he must keep up with *your* pace.

On city streets paved with asphalt or concrete, your dog's feet won't be landing as smoothly as he would like them to. For much the same reason that a car with un-aligned wheels wears out its tires faster, he will be rubbing his pads raw. In the country, it's a different story, but if your dog is attached to your bike, he can't be the sure-footed animal he would be if running free. He could very well trip on something, fall in a hole and break a leg, get something stuck between his pads, or just cut a paw, and you might not realize this until you get home and see him limping. By that time, you could have a real problem on your hands. So unless your dog is running free while you are riding, I suggest, for your dog's own safety, that you leave him at home.

A dog's leash is often the source of unexpected problems. When out shopping with your dog, be sure to watch where both he and the leash are at all times. If the end of the leash gets stuck in a closing elevator door, as the elevator begins to move, the leash will strangle him.

Almost all dogs are terrified of standing on the subway gratings. Because they feel a kind of insecurity at being suspended in midair. And at the same time, they sense the danger of catching their paws in the metalwork and breaking their knuckles. So, avoid subway gratings.

Do not take your dog on escalators where his paws can get stuck, and he could very easily lose a leg. Many a small dog has even had his knuckles broken by Gucci heels, so be careful in crowds.

You'll find in your travels that everyone you meet is not a dog lover. One girl wanted a huge Doberman for her beau, but he was afraid of dogs, especially big Dobermans, so he left her.

Another attractive miss in Manhattan adored Weimaraners and bought one for herself. Every new boyfriend would make her dump the dog. Finally she developed a whole scheme about it. She would give the dog to her friendly neighborhood restaurateur. After the affair, the man would sell it back to her.

This procedure went around four times. The restaurateur had a nice income and the girl was happy. But the problem is that individual prejudices translate themselves into law.

My wife Jo once took Inches along with her into a shop. The owner waited on her, took her money, then called the police because she had brought a dog into the store, against local regulations.

A usual sight in the park is blue-uniformed police upbraiding people for not having their dogs on a leash—a capital sin in the city. If they catch you, you're in for a fine. The word "can't" is the biggest disadvantage to dogs in the city. Can't run here, can't loiter there, can't tie up here, can't walk there.

A dog run set up by the city at 79th and Fifth Avenue is approximately 20 by 50 feet. This is hardly enough room for New York's estimated 500,000 dogs to run and play. But now that construction projects are underway, open space in all cities continues to diminish. Nor are the American parks the land of the free for dogs. They are not allowed to roam free in any state or federal campground.

I feel there ought to be more laws *for* dogs than against them. Somebody ought to find a way for dogs to exist in the city. It's a weighty problem, but well worth the effort. But besides voting for local ordinances and writing letters to your elected officials, a dog owner's best recourse is to make sure *his* animal never gives cause for offense.

A really well-trained dog should respond only to his master, or in the case of a family, to all members of the family. But a dog should be taught not to annoy or harm other people. For instance, when you have guests at your house, they are your friends and not his, so he shouldn't continually bother them. You can help your dog to understand what to do in given situations by praising him when he does the right thing. If he appears at the door and greets people nicely, praise him.

It goes without saying that your dog should be store-broken as well as housebroken. If anything happens, you're going to have to pick it up. Pets who are troublesome in stores probably have owners who are wholly ignoring them. A dog is quite able to tell when your attention is elsewhere, and may well feel that this is his chance to do as he pleases.

A man and his wife adored their husky but totally ignored her when they took her shopping. She jumped up on the counters and began rummaging through whatever was for sale. I went along as a spectator and figured out the problem instantly. Of course the husky jumped up on the counters. Her masters were so busy looking at whatever was up there that they paid no attention to the dog. She was simply introducing herself forcibly into their field of vision.

By contrast, Plum is one of the few dogs in New York City who is welcome in certain restaurants simply because he's so well behaved. At one East Side tavern I had never visited before, I quickly ordered Plum into the booth and under the table. Plum lay there, peacefully, throughout the lunch, totally concealed by the ample tablecloth. When I finally arose to leave, the waitress, who hadn't seen me or Plum come in, was clearly flabbergasted to find a sizable dog emerging from where there had been nothing but customers for the past hour.

Remember this in training your own dog. He should be a credit to his species so that *all* dogs may benefit.

20 Traveling—Cars, Kennels, and Airlines

Traveling with a dog is fraught with particular problems, which may start when you simply try to get him into the car. Most dogs love riding, and will react enthusiastically to the words "car" or "ride." But there are other dogs whose first car trip was to the veterinarian's office for inoculations or who perhaps have been startled by cars in the street, and who look on anything with four wheels as a moving Iron maiden.

You can change such a dog's attitude, but it takes a bit of time, just like getting him used to the bathtub. With the car parked and quiet, entice him at least as far as the fender, then perhaps another day into the back seat. Leave him there for a few minutes with the door open, and you in the front seat. A few days later, close the door. The next time, start the engine. Drive him first down the

driveway, later around the block, eventually on more extensive journeys, never pressing him beyond his limits. If he seems the least fearful or upset, stop and continue another time.

Once you are driving with your dog, he will enjoy sticking his nose out the window to sample the passing breeze. But there are some precautions to take into consideration. Make sure you roll the window down just enough for his muzzle to fit through, so he can't jump out. And pause and look around when push-buttoning a window *closed*. Many dogs—and children—have gotten their heads caught in exactly this way. Look before you push that button.

Teach your dog not to jump around in the car. If he were to get unruly while you were assuming any real speed, it could cause an accident. Seat belts are not for your dog, since buckling him up could lead to injury. Leashes should be removed, too, because they can catch on handles or gears and choke him. If your seats are unusually smooth, it's a good idea to provide him with a rug or mat so that his feet can enjoy some traction. Train him not to jump out of the car windows. Many dogs are killed this way. If you are not sure of him, keep the windows closed.

When you plan an extended ride with your pet, forget about feeding him beforehand. The excitement, plus the motion prolonged for an unaccustomed length of time, can make him carsick. If you must feed him, give him a fraction of what he normally eats, and plan to make frequent stops for water and leg stretching. He has to make stops just as often as you stop at the gas station.

Never leave him locked in on a warm day, since a metal car heats up very quickly, even in late afternoon sun. Whenever you park, always open the window an inch or two. But never leave it fully opened. He won't be there when you return. He'll either bolt or someone will take him. Remember, if he's very special to you, someone else is likely to see his finer qualities too. And if you leave it half open, and your dog is a husky breed like a boxer or Labrador, he may heave his way through the safety glass to attack another dog who was invading what the car-bound dog considered his turf.

Certainly your dog should never be left in the car overnight. This should be self-explanatory. A car is not a home. Ask motel management if they allow dogs before you check in. If not, they can usually assist you in finding lodging for your pet.

When I go on vacation, it's usually to a place where I can take my dogs. However, there are times that a man has to get away from his pets, just as he does from his wife. At such times, I try to have my dogs taken care of by someone who knows them and whom I can trust completely. This way I can be sure that the dogs will not be spoiled or hurt while I'm away. If I cannot find someone, then I put them in a reputable kennel. I must say that it is better to put them in a good kennel than to leave them with an irresponsible person.

Give your dog the consideration he deserves and remember that he is not a car to be put in dead storage for any length of time but rather a living creature for whom you are responsible. Don't wait to the last minute to make arrangements. Just as in the better hotels, the better kennels fill up very quickly. If you end up settling for the wrong kennel, your dog might come back with worms, kennel cough, ticks, or just about anything.

Before you choose a kennel, check with your vet and also with people who have had satisfactory dealings with a particular kennel. Best of all, go out and check the kennel yourself. Don't go out there announced, but make a surprise visit, preferably during the week because many people visit on weekends. Advertisements in newspapers and magazines mean nothing. The only way to find out about a kennel is by checking it personally. Your dog cannot report on the conditions, so you have to make sure that they are right.

Make sure that the kennel is clean, that is has adequate exercising areas, and most of all, make sure it has competent help, with a veterinarian on call twenty-four hours a day. Ask for the vet's name and speak with him personally if you can. If you go to a kennel that holds approximately sixty dogs and you only see one person in help, it is obvious that he can't possibly take care of them all. Check that there is adequate heating and proper ventilation. Make sure you know what he will be fed, because a swift change in diet can cause diarrhea, or a loss of appetite and therefore a loss in weight.

Don't forget that when you send your dog to a boarding kennel, he won't be let free to roam. He will be put in a cage or pen and *should* be taken out for a walk three or four times a day. This is why it is so important that the cages be of adequate size and very clean, and why there should be enough help and runs to insure your dog of getting his needed exercise.

If the dogs share pens or exercise areas, make sure that the kennel has a policy on pack systems for grouping. In other words, make sure they don't put two mature males together, as this will almost certainly insure a fight. Make sure they don't board heated females under any circumstances because one female in heat can upset an entire kennel. If you have a heated female or one that is nearing heat, try to cancel your vacation till the heat's over. When you find a good kennel, stick with it, because this will give your dog a feeling of security through familiarity.

If you are going where you *can* take a dog, there's no need to kennel him up. Basically a dog can adjust to any given situation. The husky, a dog originally bred to survive outdoors in −60 degrees, has adapted comfortably to Florida and Hawaii. If you can stand your vacation spot, your dog probably can too.

Of all the transportation problems your dog may face, however, the most serious is that of the airplane. Many a dog panics while stored in the cargo area of an airliner. Frightened by the noise, movement, and temperature changes, the dog can become terror stricken and thrash about, biting everything in sight.

My pet peeve with the airlines is that they seldom exert any real control over the air shipment of animals. Many an animal has been harassed, maimed, or killed during shipment. Poor ventilation in cargo holds, inadequate crates, and of course neglect by the handlers, shippers, and airlines themselves are the main causes.

United Airlines reports that it carried some fifty thousand dogs during 1972. About thirty died en route, but it estimates that ten of these would have perished regardless of handling. "Some dogs are just unsuited for traveling and they become very excited, agitated, and perish from heart attacks or other nervous causes." Therefore, I recommend that, if your dog tends to be nervous, think twice before shipping him by air. A tranquilizer may be the answer, but ask your vet if it is advisable for your particular dog.

Heat and ventilation seem to be the main problems.

As we've seen, a dog's lack of sweat makes him particularly prone to overheating. "Dogs are critically hot when their body temperature reaches 106 degrees and 109 degrees could be fatal," says the United Airlines report. "Typically, overheating occurs because the baggage compartment of the aircraft gets too hot as a result of delays on the ground."

Most baggage compartments designed for carrying live animals are heated and pressurized, but not air-conditioned. "If the baggage compartment gets hot while the aircraft is on the ground, it will not be cooled," the airlines report continues. "On the other hand, when the plane is in flight, the temperature of the outside air is low enough to activate the heating system and keep the compartment at a comfortable temperature."

In the DC-10, temperature ranges between 40 degrees and 80 degrees Fahrenheit—usually between 50 and 70 degrees. In Yuma, Arizona, when the outside ground temperature is 80 degrees, the cargo pit heated to 91 to 95 degrees. Thirty minutes later, at 29,000 feet with an outside temperature of –45 degrees, cargo-pit temperatures ranged from 89 to 92 degrees. Fifteen minutes later they were down to 76 to 84 degrees.

In the 737, the temperature in the pit designated for live animals ranges between 30 degrees and 70 degrees—usually between 35 and 50 degrees. This would also typify temperature ranges in other Boeing equipment. On the 747 the compartment is ventilated, heated, and air-conditioned while in flight. "Consequently, it is probably the most comfortable compartment for the transportation of dogs that we have. *Note,* however, that while the aircraft is on the ground, this baggage compartment is not air-conditioned."

Airlines recommend that "when people ship their dogs during the hot summer months, they choose late night or early morning flights." Don't ship females while they're in heat at any time of year. If there is one female in heat in a baggage compartment, any male dogs can hurt themselves in their energetic attempts to reach her.

Make sure that the dog is in a proper size kennel. One Borzoi, a prize show dog that weighed 120 pounds, was put into a kennel designed for an 80-pound dog on the advice of a professional dog handler. The dog died, and now at least one set of airline regulations do not accept a dog weighing more than 80 pounds.

The way the kennel is loaded into the plane is also crucial. No more than one-third of the pit should be loaded. Air space must be left so that there can be some circulation and ventilation. If there is dry ice nearby, it will evaporate and produce carbon dioxide, and the dog will suffocate—a particular problem with boxers, bulldogs, and others with short snouts.

After reading over all these facts it still boils down to one thing: Dog-owning passengers should apply common sense when shipping the pets and always remember that animals are *not* baggage, but living, breathing creatures. It is up to you to ensure the safety of your pet.

If you do have to fly with your dog, it's not a bad idea to buy or build a strong, properly ventilated crate. Don't use a cage, because you want your dog to see as little as possible of what's going on. A full view of the baggage-room circus will make him very nervous. He needs as much closed-in feeling as he can possibly get. More importantly, the more familiar his crate seems to him, the better he'll adjust to it.

In choosing your flight, remember that every additional stop guarantees more loading and unloading and drastic temperature changes. Try to book your dog through nonstop. Make sure no baggage is stacked on top of the kennel, or it could collapse, crushing your dog.

A tranquilizer, if recommended by your vet, isn't a bad idea, but it won't calm your dog nearly as effectively as getting him used to his crate a week or so before the actual flight time. As you did when getting him used to a car, introduce him to his crate in slow, simple stages—preferably when he's sleepy, so that he will relax automatically and even tend to doze off whenever he's inside. Leave him in there for as long as the flight is supposed to be. When you let him out again, praise him and play with him, let him stretch his muscles and show him everything's all right.

These precautions, plus some advance planning with airline personnel, should insure you a happy, healthy pet when you get wherever you're headed. But it is up to *you* to make sure that he is going to make a pleasant adjustment.

Again, consider potentially new sights and sounds.

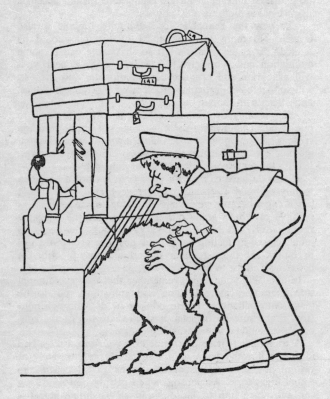

When I brought two young Mexican hairless dogs up north, they had never seen rain before. It seemed to hypnotize them. They would stand perfectly still, as if in a trance, then suddenly keel over. The fall to the ground would snap them out of it.*

It never hurts to check out the local wildlife. I once took my dogs to Canada just in time for the annual hatch of fish flies. By the time the tent was up, the dogs were being driven frantic by the clouds of otherwise harmless insects.

Another travel problem is medical attention. While traveling in South Dakota, Snap, one of my Maltese, had her ear stung by a wasp. A hospital trip was necessary, so I drove twenty miles to the nearest veterinarian, who specialized in cattle and who was not in when we arrived. I had to drive to the vet's home and ferry him back to his office.

The doctor then discovered he didn't have one of those stainless steel gizmos small enough to look in the ears of a Maltese. The one he had for the cattle was obviously way out of scale. Finally they borrowed one from a neighboring pediatrician. The vet then admitted he was afraid that Snap might bite him. Though reassured, he was still jittery about hurting her, seeing as he had never worked on "such a little thing." But he finally treated the wasp bite and submitted a bill for four dollars—a pittance when you figure out the miles, house, and patience involved. But I was even luckier to have found a veterinarian at all.

People at summer beach houses have been known to leash their dogs on the porch. Not such a good idea if the beach house is built on more than one level, because all a leashed dog has to do is jump off the porch and he's hung himself. This happens all the time. But all this doesn't mean you shouldn't take your faithful companion with you on a vacation. Just prepare for possible emergencies and make sure you take the extra time to show your dog what the place is like.

Thousands of dogs have made the fretful transition from Connecticut farmland to teeming Manhattan, but one well-behaved cocker spaniel turned into a barking dog over-

* Dogs can be hypnotized, but not in the way humans can. A flashlight beam in their faces at night or something rhythmic and unfamiliar can leave them rooted to the spot.

night. It seems that the family had moved in for the summer, right next door to some sort of professional massage parlor. People would come in all hours of the day and night. Since he came from a very quiet, sedate home, the dog couldn't put up with that much traffic. I overcame the situation by having the owners keep the dog outside many hours of the night, saying "no" every time he got upset about a new visitor."

In the transition from city to country, the same problem is often encountered. A dog unaccustomed to the noise of farm and wild animals must be shown in the same manner that there is no danger.

When making the move to a new home, be it permanent or temporary, you must introduce the dog to it just as you would a child. If you simply throw the dog into the kitchen or bathroom, he will panic. Animals, like people, fear the unknown. Therefore, take him with you around the house for the first few days. You must show your dog that nothing has changed except the surroundings.

Your dog has no smells of his own urine in the new place—so keep it that way. Dogs can forget all about being housebroken when moving to a new home, so make sure that he is on a leash and not out of your sight for a few days. This will insure that he cannot pick up any bad habits.

For the first night it is a good idea to let him sleep in the bedroom with you. After your dog gets used to the house, confine him to a small area as you did when housebreaking him. Once he adjusts, give him his freedom. If he makes a mistake, reprimand him for it with the vinegar method. The same obedience is expected of him— nothing less and maybe something more.

Part Three

BASIC OBEDIENCE TRAINING

21 Basic Training— for You

In the park, I once met a woman in her sixties whose dog was playing amiably with other canines. All of a sudden she barked, *"Come, King"* in a voice that would have befitted an army drill sergeant.

She explained that the dog had been trained by a man with a deep voice and the dog would respond to her only if she shouted in this manner. I told her that certain trainers believe that a deep, loud voice is necessary in getting dogs to obey, but this is not so—she could retrain her dog to her own natural voice if she wanted. I think this particular woman likes having an extra range to her vocal chords. However, when dog owners ask me what tone of voice to use in giving commands to their dogs, I tell them to use their normal tone.

There is no magic in the male voice. One woman told me that her dog only responds to men because of their deep voices. I told her dog to "stay" in a high falsetto, and he did. As long as he's trained, your dog will respond. I have even helped people, with their larynx removed, to have well-behaved animals.

Repetition and authority are very important. One of the big secrets is doing whatever exercise you want the dog to do over and over. Gradually he accepts it as something you want him to do, and does it.

A dog likes to win your approval, and so you should give him plenty of opportunities to please you. Your dog *enjoys* performing tricks once he's got them down pat, simply for the praise and pleasure he elicits from you. If you got him to make you happy in the first place, let him do what he's here for.

I remind clients never to lose their temper with a dog. When you lose your temper, either physically or verbally, your gestures aren't always methodical and simple. Jumping around in anger will only scare your dog. He will become extremely confused and therefore very reluctant to respond in your training sessions, since he never knows what your reactions might be. Shouters are the kind of people whose dogs never really get disciplined, simply because the owners haven't any discipline themselves.

The rule that a dog should be corrected immediately has few exceptions. One is if your dog urinates while you are training him at something other than housebreaking. Don't confuse him with reprimands. He's liable to associate his punishment with whatever you are trying to teach him, and will thus refuse to obey. Finish his basic lesson first. When he's got the idea, *then* wait at least half an hour before dragging him over to clean up the mess.

When training, assume your dog is *already* perfect. This way, his smallest goof will come glaringly to your attention, and you will be much less likely to let it slip by. If a dog does know what he's supposed to do and still doesn't follow instructions, the original mistake was yours, not his. Once you slip up, your dog is guaranteed to foul up on his own. Be honest with yourself, however, on how well trained you *really* want your dog to be. A Swedish lady was so proud of the work she had done with her Doberman that she invited me to come up to the country to watch her put the dog through his paces. The woman was very militaristic in her training, and her dog was impeccable. Actually his behavior was a little stiff for normal living, but to this particular woman he was a model dog.

At the other extreme are hopelessly ill-trained dogs whose owners really don't mind and genuinely seem to enjoy the anarchy and confusion. So, there's no point in training your dog to do more than you really care about. Once you are basically satisfied with him, your motivation will taper off. You won't correct him as promptly, be as disappointed when he fails or regresses, and your training will be largely a waste of time. It's up to you, ultimately, to decide what "ideal" behavior really is.

Once you have decided, only one person should be the last word on dog discipline. If everyone in your family has a different idea of what discipline is, your dog will only grow confused. Your dog's commands should be taught by one person at a time. Of course, eventually wife, husband, and child can give the dog the same commands, but it's best to wait until the dog has learned the command from the first person who taught him.

Gear the length of a lesson to the dog's attention span. One little boy wanted to know why his cocker spaniel was so tired after a lesson. I told him it's because he's a very young puppy and the lessons were too long and exhausting to him. Next year this same dog will be big and strong enough to take fifteen- or twenty-minute lessons, but right now, his attention span is too short. It tires him out just to listen and try to make the right connections. How would you teach a very young child? Everything has to be made plain and simple but still interesting, doesn't it? This is doubly true with a dog. The shorter the time you spend on lessons, the quicker and the better your puppy will respond. Five minutes of training three or four times a day is a reasonable schedule.

Yes, it does take patience, but it's worth it in the long run. If you work with your dog too much at one time, he'll get bored and tired. He will think of the training session as a punishment, and nothing will be accomplished. He won't want to work with you, and you'll have a hard time getting him to respond to any of your commands. How would you like to do things that are continually boring or unpleasant?

Always play with your dog before and right after an exercise. Show him you're pleased. If you want to give him treats, give them to him before or after an exercise. He should respond to you because *you* want him to and not for a food reward. If you reward him during the exercise, his mind will be on the food and not on the exercise. He will therefore get so excited that he won't do the exercise properly. This is always true.

The times set down above are primarily for puppy work, since the puppy stage is the best time to inculcate discipline. On older dogs, increase the training exercise periods to about fifteen minutes, at least once a day. If you work with him several times a day, give him a few hours' break in between. But when you're not working with him, be his friend. Hug him, pat him, do all those things the owners do in the dog-food commercials.

Dogs respond to love just as humans do, flourishing in loving surroundings.

My training follows a precise sequence. First of all, you should train your dog in exercises that can be performed indoors, getting him used to the leash and your commands *before* he goes outside. I do recommend, however, that you teach your dog these exercises in the exact order given here. Lying down and sitting for instance, are so similar that a dog can easily get confused if taught them in quick succession. Or, worse, he can begin to anticipate your command. If, several times running, you tell him to sit, then lie, there's a good chance he'll decide to make things easier by eliminating what to him seems like the middle step, and you'll have a dog that lies down when told simply to sit. It's better that each command be separate and distinct in his mind before you begin linking them together.

"Sit" and "stay" should be taught at the same time. We assume "no" has already been drummed into his head. Then teach the command "come," as he should know this as early as possible, and only then "lie down" and "heel." All these commands should be taught in this order, either on a leash or in a confined area, until perfect control is shown. Then, after you have perfect control of the basic commands both by voice and hand, you can teach your dog to come to you outside and to heel off a leash.

Your first investments should be a collar and training leash. They aren't absolutely indispensable for training work, at least not at first, but they do help even the most obedient dog understand much quicker that you're boss. You will definitely need a leash and collar for later training, and for going outside. If you have any doubts about controlling your dog during a training session, the leash will eliminate them. Get the problem of adjusting him to a lead over with, so you can devote your full attention to having him obey.

I see no justification for the spiked training collars that are frequently sold, which bite into the dog's neck at the slightest tug of the leash. I have only one, which I removed from a client's dog who didn't need it. In all leash training, it's not pulling but jerking that lets the dog know what you want of him. There are some exceptions, which we'll cover later, but even so, a dog must not be punished by an abrasive collar while he's performing the *right* thing.

The best training collar is a simple synthetic fiber "choke" with a ring at each end. Simply loop the chord through either metal ring, and enlarge the resulting loop to fit your dog's neck. The leash is then attached to the free ring. Be sure, however, that the choke forms a straight line as it leaves your dog's neck, passes through the ring, and continues on to the leash. This way, the choke will automatically loosen when you give it slack. If the choke turns a corner as it leaves the ring, the collar will bind and remain tight after your first jerk on the leash.

To make training as easy as possible, it helps to have *some* collar on your dog from the beginning, and if he is already wearing one, you should leave it on him. A dog who has worn a collar for some time seems to consider it a part of himself. When a dog's long-worn collar is removed for a bath or replacement, he will often act sheepish and submissive, almost as a human would if caught on Main Street in his shorts. After a while, dogs apparently consider the collar the link to which their master's leash, and thus their master, is attached to them, and it may even provide a sense of security.

In selecting a training leash, length is the most important factor. Some owners, who want to give their dogs free rein and still comply with city ordinances about unleashed pets, invest in a 150-yard clothesline. If a dog is allowed to run in the park, the final result resembles Charlie Brown's kite. Even the standard ten-foot leash is a bit much. A six-foot leash is long enough for your dog to move about easily, but still short enough for you to control him.

When a family is participating in the training exercises, remember that only one member should work an exercise at one time, and that no one must interfere or the dog will get completely confused. If you don't really want to work the exercises yourself, let another member of the family do it. Otherwise you probably won't be consistent and will do the exercise wrong.

At first don't try to train your dog where there are too many distractions. But after the dog starts to respond, then do start to introduce outside distractions. This will help to reinforce the training, and the dog will learn to listen to you even in the face of a hurricane, if need be.

To recapitulate:

1. *Don't yell. Speak in your normal tone of voice.*
2. *Always use hand signals along with verbal commands.*
3. *Stay calm, and never lose your temper.*
4. *Be methodical. Don't make the mistake of trying to correct a hundred sins simultaneously.*
5. *Be consistent. Your dog has to know that you are pleased only when he does the right things.*
6. *Be authoritative. Don't expect him to just pick up the life-style you desire him to have, show him how you want him to behave. This is the humane thing to do.*

7. *Be firm. He must learn to accept the fact that his way is not divine. Remember, there's no way but yours. He will not always get his way and may not even get it at all.*

8. *Be patient. Sooner or later, he'll think what you've taught him is the only way.*

9. *Last but not least: after he's done what you want, give him plenty of loving. Your dog lives for praise and affection. The most important message you have for him is that you are his master, that you do love him and will not do him any harm.*

22 "Sit" and "Stay"

A young lovely in New York City took her two brand-new cockers with her on a shopping spree before they were trained. She tied them to a chair in a restaurant while she visited the ladies' room, and came back to behold the chair being dragged through the restaurant, knocking over everything in its wake. Silverware and glasses were flying.

While in a store, one not-so-bright mother bid her daughter hold on to their big Dalmatian. Seconds later, the Dalmatian was ripping through the store, knocking down dress racks and whatever fell into its course, the daughter screaming wildly behind.

Even if you *haven't* covered "no," the very first commands you should teach your dog are to sit and stay. These are both stationary commands and pose less possible confusion than the others. When you take your dog for a walk, you will be especially grateful if he's got this preliminary training down pat, and equally sorry if he hasn't.

Put the collar and leash on your dog and take him to a convenient corner in your home. The reason for using a corner in the first place is to keep him in a somewhat restricted area, so as to make his escape less likely. After all, he's surrounded on three sides, by the walls on two and you on the third. It is also very important for you to remember exactly where the sit/stay spot is, so that you can bring him back to it with accuracy. This eliminates confusion for the very young pup and even for the older dog getting his first lesson in obedience.

144

Don't take him to a corner where there is a lot of racket, however. A sharp noise could go off at the same time you give the word "sit." The dog could then learn to associate the command with the noise and might never learn what it really means. You could tell him to sit until you're blue in the face, and he will never respond.

Once he's standing in the corner, do three things all at once:

- *Point to the floor with one hand. (Don't point to his tail because there are no eyes on that end.)*
- *With your other hand, jerk back on the leash or push down on his hindquarters to force him into a sitting position.*
- *Say "sit," once.*

This three-part procedure is basic for all commands. As we've seen, hand commands are a very important part of obedience training. Always use the hand command at the same time you give the verbal command, so that your dog will learn both commands simultaneously. Usually a dog will learn hand commands faster than voice, and if after the first lesson you merely point to a sit position, the dog will usually do it. If you say "sit" without the hand commands, however, chances are he won't.

If he doesn't sit for you, drop the leash and push him to a sitting position, again saying "sit" at the same time. Remember that you're *not* reprimanding your dog, just teaching him to sit. Be patient, give all commands in your normal tone of voice, and finish what you start. You should not call your dog by name when teaching him this or any new command. "Spot, sit," "stay, Spot" will tend to confuse him. Just say "sit," or the command for whatever you are teaching him. But *after* you teach him the command and he is responding to it, then it is all right to use his name before a command.

People who have trouble getting their dogs to obey should name them Stop, Stay, Come, or Go. A really undone person could name his dog No.

Both sitting and staying commands have to be taught together. If not, you will be running all over the house telling your dog to sit. "Stay" will keep him in position while you go over to pat him and praise him, a very important element in all training.

When your dog sits for you, praise him. Then immediately push your hand straight toward him, palm out, like a police officer stopping traffic. At the same time, say "stay," once.

Immediately turn away and don't look back until you're about ten feet from him. Then turn around and face him.

If he is staying, praise him. If you are one of the vast majority of owners, however, you will probably find that he's either following you or has run off in some other direction. Wait until he gets to where he's going. Then go to him, get a firm grip on him, without saying a word, and give him a firm shake, saying "no."

The misplaced "no" is one of the chief errors in sit/stay training. Even if you see him getting up immediately, you must turn your back and walk several paces off. If you reprimand him as soon as he starts to get up, he's apt to associate the "no" with the very thing you were teaching him to do. Don't stop him in the middle of running away, but let him go to wherever he feels secure, whether it be under the bed or at your feet. Then get him and put him back on the sit/stay spot. Whenever you have to go and get him back, say "no," and then repeat the sit-and-stay command all over again.

The reason that you must allow him to get to his security spot before going to bring him back is to teach him that there is no security but with you or in doing what you tell him. This will not break his spirit or make him insecure or even nervous, but will merely place him in a position to be very responsive to accurate training. You will find that he will soon gain a new confidence once he knows what is expected of him.

Take him back to the exact corner where you just told him to stay. Repeat the command *once*, again holding your palm up before his muzzle as if to push him. Again walk away. Repeat this procedure until he gets tired of being told "no" and taken back to the corner.

It is extremely important that you bring him back each time to the same exact spot where you told him to sit and stay in the first place. He must learn that when you say something you mean exactly that. He must learn to sit and stay where you want.

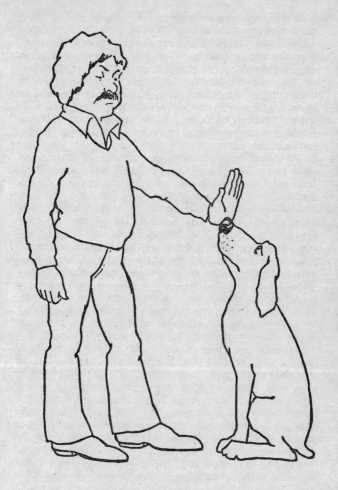

When he finally stays, give him lots of praise. Many trainers suggest rewarding the dog with food whenever he behaves satisfactorily, but it's really not necessary. For elementary training, your praise is reward enough. He's supposed to understand that he *must* obey, rewards or not, and besides, the smell of dog biscuits can be distracting to an eager puppy. If you must use food to reward your dog, use it only after a training session or for very difficult tricks, such as the jumping and magazine-fetching variety, where an extra incentive is needed beyond mere praise.

But remember your dog *must* remain in that corner until you release him. Now that he is still sitting there, hold your hand out in the "stay" position as you did before and say "good boy." "Stay." Walk toward your dog, not saying another word, but holding your hand out in front of you in the stay position. Go all the way over to him and touch him, saying "good boy." Then immediately give him the voice and hand command "stay." Remember that you do not say anything to him before you touch him as he might consider this to be a release from the command. Practice this exercise until your dog responds immediately to both voice and hand commands. Once he does this, you are ready to vary the sit-and-stay exercise and take him to spots other than a corner. Some of my clients' dogs are so well-trained that when they are given a command they stop whatever they're doing and respond immediately. They have to be released to do any other action. It's a joy to watch.

Always remember to give your dog a relaxing remark so he'll know *exactly* when he is released from his command. After he is obeying the command "stay," take hold of the leash and jerk it gently toward you, giving him whatever word you choose to release him from the command. Something like the army command "at ease." When you say "good boy," he should remain in the corner just sitting. The release word should be something else.

However, it may be a mistake to use "okay" as your release word if this term occurs frequently in your conversation as it does in mine. Oftentimes I'll give Plum a command such as sit-and-stay. Then someone will ask me something, and if I answer with an okay, Plum takes it as his release word and is gone. This happens because once he has been given a command, he listens carefully to whatever I say thereafter. When I say "okay," he naturally thinks I am talking to him.

Perhaps the best release "word" is a hand signal such as patting your thigh or clapping your hands, both of which can also double as joyful commands to come. But whatever your choice of signal, always use it when you've finished exercising him so he knows it's all right to go back to normal dog life.

Before leaving, however, make sure he completes any exercise you start. This is one of the most basic points in training. Once you start a command, you must carry through with it even if you must physically carry your animal through the paces.

A dog is not supposed to do anything else, and should not be trained to do anything else, until the initial lesson is completed. If for any reason you are interrupted in the midst of a training session, *go back to it as soon as possible*. Otherwise, the next time you command him, your dog may feel that an interruption means he doesn't have to obey, and he will dawdle, waiting for the bell, telephone, or door that means class is over. Remember that you are the one he learns from, and if he doesn't learn it right, it is your fault and not his. If you can get the script and movements down pat, your dog will obey and do as you command.

The sit-and-stay commands should be worked separately from all other commands until they are perfect. Never mix basic commands together until each one is perfect by itself. But once he is really perfect in the corner, put his leash on and take him to the center of the room so that there are no restrictions around him. Place him on your *left* side with his front legs right beside yours, and close enough to you that his right shoulder is actually touching your left leg. Without turning around, bring your right arm across so that it is in front of your dog and pointing down to the floor, tell him to sit.

Do this once only. If he refuses to sit, jerk the leash backward, thus forcing him to sitting position. If he still won't sit, push him down. Praise him when he sits, but make sure he does not get up. Immediately drop the leash and change your hand command from the sit command to a stay command, at the same time saying "stay." Say "stay" only once, then immediately walk away.

Follow the exact same procedure you did when first teaching your dog the sit/stay commands in the corner. If he runs away, let him go, and get him only after he has reached his security spot. Then reprimand him and return him to the place where you told him to sit and stay. If he stays, return to your dog. But this time, walk around him until you are at his side in the same position as when you gave him the command to sit and stay. Only then should he be released.

Once he can do this, you can start to make things a little more difficult for him. First of all, make him sit and stay, then leave the room. After that come back in and walk around him. He must learn that "stay" means *stay*. When he is proficient at this exercise try it with as many distractions as possible.

It is particularly important that he learn to sit and stay with other dogs around. Most obedience trials have an exercise in which he must do this for varying lengths of time either in your presence or with you leaving and then returning, but always with other dogs in the vicinity.

The very distractions that *do* make him leave the sit/stay position are the ones you should work on. Try to build up the amount of time he will sit and stay without moving. At the same time try to use just your hand commands to get him to sit and stay. Remember that most of the obedience trials allow only either voice or hand commands, but not both.

If your dog breaks the sit-and-stay because of any of these distractions, you *must* start all over and make him go through with it properly before praising and releasing him. Otherwise, he will simply learn that distractions are an excuse for disobedience.

Let him get where he is going and then reprimand him, saying "no" very firmly; but *never* punish a dog when teaching him, or he will come to associate the punishment with the command. Therefore, he will never respond but will, in fact, run away because he thinks he is going to get punished when he hears that command. Simply drag him back to his sit position and continue doing this until he learns that "no" means no, "sit" means sit, and "stay" means stay.

Sounds repetitious? Of course it is, but the results can surprise you. One set of Afghans were so well-disciplined that they once sat for a full hour awaiting their master's permission to move again. He had not said "okay," the local magic words, and they clung to the original order. That is discipline! And once your dog begins approaching this level of excellence, you'll be ready to teach him to come when called—his most important obedience lesson, indoors or out.

23 "Come"

In my opinion, the command "come" is the most important of all the commands that your dog can learn. When he has mastered this command, you can have complete confidence that, no matter what, he will always return to your side when you want him to do so. Once he learns this command perfectly, he is ready to perform the more complex ones, as he is now under your control at all times.

At the same time, learning to come gives him the security of knowing that, until you call him, he is free to roam without being uncertain as to what's expected of him.

The best, and easiest, time to get your dog to respond to the command "come" is between the ages of six weeks and four months. Indians knew and used this principle when training their dogs. They carried their puppies with them constantly from as early an age as possible. This way the dog learned to look on them as a parent figure and obey them completely. This type of behavior in animals is known as imprinting, and it seems to be an inborn instinctive process on which an animal's survival depends. Animals must learn as early as possible where their protection lies and thus to what species they belong. But a dog's critical marking period, during which time he will readily accept new masters, is over at about thirteen weeks. It has been proved that a pup who has never been in contact with humans before the age of thirteen weeks never learns to relate to them and is almost impossible to keep as a pet. He will consider himself a dog and will take "orders" only from other dogs.

After this age, *any* dog will be more set in his ways and affections. This is not to say that an older dog can't be taught new tricks, it just takes longer and more reinforcement. So it's impossible to overstress the advantage you have by training your dog during this critical period. Try to get as much training in at as early an age as possible.

The first place to start teaching your dog to come is in a confined area, such as your house or apartment, where there is no possibility of his running away from you. Put a six-foot training leash on him without giving him any commands at all. Then, holding him at leash-length away from you, pull him toward you, using the command "come."

While you are pulling on the leash, which should always be held in your left hand, motion for him to come to you with your right hand, in a large beckoning gesture.* (Many people pat their thighs. But select only one gesture for any command, and stick to it.) Make sure that each time you reel him in to you, he is given lots of praise.

After he comes to you with only a slight jerk on the leash, call him to you before actually jerking it. He will begin to associate the word "come" with your beckoning gesture and with the jerk on his leash. Once he starts to come with only the slightest jerk, then try saying "come" without pulling on the leash at all.

Once he comes without a jerk on the leash, however, don't stop pulling completely. Alternate the times you gesture, say "come," and *don't* pull the leash with the times that you do. This will serve to reinforce his obeying the command. Remember to train in five-minute intervals only, and to make sure you complete each repetition of the exercise. Whether he does it well or not—even if you have to reel him in—he must come every time you tell him to do so.

When your dog learns to come without your having to jerk on the leash at all, take your set of house keys in your right hand. Holding the leash with your left, gently flip the keys directly at your dog, making sure they hit him. Just after, but not as soon as they hit him, tell him to come, using your beckoning gesture.

If he doesn't come immediately, jerk on the leash, and if he still doesn't come, reel him in. Make sure you use only a one-word command, in this case, the word "come," and that you give the command only once and then

---

* This is the traditional method and most effective.

make him respond. Repeat this exercise until the dog comes to you when you merely drop the keys near him.

The purpose of the keys is to give you some kind of control in the next step of the "come" command, which is to have him obey when off the leash. The keys let him know that, no matter where he is, you can reach him. It is the same idea as taking away your dog's security spot, as you did during his sit/stay training. He must always be chased from his hiding places and have keys lobbed at him when he refuses to come. *You* must be his source of security.

I was once employed by a crippled lady who walked with crutches and couldn't handle two English spaniels on leashes. But she could certainly throw keys, first in the house, to establish her dominant position, and then later outside. I suggested she bang one crutch, since this was one "weapon" she would always have handy, indoors or out, to throw fear into her recalcitrant spaniels. The crutch made a nice booming sound, and eventually her dogs would freeze when they heard the noise, convinced that she could reach them at any distance. Eventually the dogs learned to come whenever she tapped her crutch sharply on the sidewalk.

Once you have your dog responding to keys, you can begin to train him off the leash. Do this at first only in a confined area such as your home. At your convenience, and when he is involved in other things, call your dog. If he does not come, throw the keys. This will teach him to respond immediately in any situation.

Never let any other people interfere while you are training. For instance, oftentimes another person will try to encourage your dog to respond to you by saying, "Go on over to him, that's a good boy." The dog will then go to that person as protection because he is being praised by him. Too many voices can confuse the dog, and only one person should give the command at a time. If he comes, praise him *after* he comes all the way to you. Pat him as you praise him. If he doesn't come, throw the keys at him, and after they hit, call him again.

A very important note to remember is that, if you throw the keys and he still doesn't come, you must not run after him screaming, *"Come!"* If you do this, it will only panic him, or he will make a game out of running away from you.

You must be quiet and methodical. If he runs away, wait until he stops and go after him. Get as close as you can to him. If possible, hit him with your keys and tell him "no." Then turn around and walk away from him, back to the spot where you called him from, even if it is in a different room, and call him again.

Even if he follows you, you must walk away a few feet before turning around and calling him. When he comes all the way to you, praise him.

If he still won't come, then go and get him, saying the word "no," which he should understand very well by now. Put the leash on him and take him to the spot where you called him from. Then praise him. Repeat and repeat until he comes every time you call him. In fact, he must learn to respond in this way merely to the sound of the keys. No matter how annoying or disobedient your dog is, the only reprimands you must give him are the thrown keys and the word "no." *You cannot hit him when you finally get him back.* That is why, when I throw the keys, I say "come" only after they hit.

He must always feel it is good to come when you call him. Too many people have a tendency to call their dog when they want to punish him. When the dog does something wrong in the house, they say, "Come here, you little bastard," or, "Come here; why did you do that?" They then punish him. He thus learns not to come when called, and this could be fatal if he is in danger and you try to call him. His response will be to run the other way. No matter how angry you are with your dog, don't ever punish him when he comes, or you might as well forget this entire exercise.

By the same token, don't ever commiserate with your dog if he has done the wrong thing, even if it is not his fault. I once showed a client the correct way to reprimand his dog. However, the dog associated the area in which he had been reprimanded with the reprimand itself. A few days later, the three of us were walking in that very area. The owner again called his dog over to him. But instead of obeying, the dog took off.

The owner got very angry and started yelling at him, but when I explained why the animal was afraid of that area, the owner became very apologetic. When he finally got the dog back, he praised him. The dog, naturally

felt that the praise was for running away, and he will do it
with more confidence in the future.

"Come" is an extremely touchy command, requiring the
most work of any of the basic commands, so the best
thing you can do is start working it with your dog from the
very beginning. The main reason I like to work with dogs
at a very early age is because at this point they can't run
too fast, and I can catch up with them easily.

Go back a step once in a while to review. Even when
he is perfect, he must be taken back a few steps and reminded once in a while. While practicing this exercise in
the house, try to use distractions such as other dogs.
Call him when he is really involved in playing with another dog and make sure that he comes to you immediately. Responding immediately under these circumstances
is the test he must pass before you can try him off the leash
outside.

Remember that he must be perfect in one stage before
going on to the next. Many people make the mistake of
letting a dog loose outside before he is controllable. Then,
since all dogs like the idea of being free, he will never
come back until he feels like it.

24 "Lie Down"

It is best to hold off teaching your dog to lie down until after you have him coming to you on command. This way, you stand a better chance of not having him confuse the command with "sit" or "stay." The three are fairly similar, after all, so it's better to separate these commands in time so that he understands they are separate and distinct.

The "down" command is a relatively easy one, but for some strange reason, it tends to be something many dogs are obstinate about. Often you will find that when you tell your dog to sit and stay, after a while he will get tired and lie down, but when you *tell* him to lie down, he will refuse. Make sure that your dog learns that you mean what you say, and that "sit" means sit *only*.

Teaching the dog to lie down is a much easier operation than "come." Most of the teachings are relatively easy. They just eat up a lot of your patience.

The first thing to do is to sit yourself down comfortably on the floor facing your dog, who should also be sitting. Place one hand on his upper back and the other behind the lower part of his front legs. Give the command "down," and at the same time, push down on his back and pull his legs out from under him—very carefully so that he doesn't think he's going to get hurt.

As soon as he is lying down, say "good boy" and praise him. In a dog's mind, being pushed is an aggressive act on your part; you're pushing him into submission. Therefore, do it very slowly and gently so that he doesn't panic. I don't advise that you try this with a full-grown strange dog, as you could get bitten. Make sure that he knows you well before doing this, and have him well trained in obeying the sit-and-stay commands and accustomed to obeying you.

Once he is lying down and you have praised him, push him back up into a sitting position, but without giving the command for him to sit. Then repeat the same thing over and over, until he lies down with only a slight pressure on his back.

At this point you can feel sure that he has some idea of what the command "down" means and is ready for the next step. Put him in a sitting position. Hook your left thumb under his collar, and turn your right hand palm down. Move your hand straight down to the floor in front of him, thus showing the dog the direction you want him to go. At the same time give the voice command "down," and pull down on his collar with a firm steady pressure. Do not jerk on the collar, and make sure that you keep the hand with which you gave the command down on the floor in front of him.

Once he is down, remove your thumb from the collar and with your right hand give him the "stay" command. Then after he is staying, praise him.

Continue this exercise, gradually exerting less and less pressure on the collar. Once he responds with no pressure on the collar whatsoever, then you know that he has associated your word and hand commands with the act of lying down. At this point just give him the command once. If he refuses, then exert pressure. This exercise is complete only after he responds on the first voice or hand command of "down."

When teaching your dog to lie down, it is most important to remember three things. First of all, once he starts to lie down on his own, release the pressure that you exert on him. Secondly, as soon as your dog actually reaches the down position, always release your hand command for "down" and change it to a "stay" command. If you don't do this, he will probably roll over on his back, a submissive gesture, in response to your aggressive act of pushing him down. Thirdly, don't keep repeating, "Down, down, down," while you try to get him to lie down. As in all commands, say it only once. In this command, however, it is a good idea to say "dowwwwn" in a long-drawn-out tone, to let it sink in. Continue this pronunciation until he learns the word and then you can say it in your normal way.

Now he is ready to learn to respond to this command when you are in a standing position. Put on his six-foot training leash, and tell your dog to sit and stay. Take hold of the leash and put it under the arch space of your shoe just between the sole and heel of your shoe where the leash will slide freely back and forth. Then stand up straight, holding the end of the leash in your left hand.

At this point one end of the leash should be attached to his collar, the other end should be in your left hand, and the middle of it should be under your shoe. With your right hand, make the "down" motion, and at the same time tell him "dowwwwn."

If he does lie down, priase him and make him stay. If he refuses, repeat the hand and voice command, but this time exert a slow steady pressure by pulling up on the leash. The leash will then "feed" through the arch of your shoe and force him down. Keep your hand in the downward position until he reaches the floor.

Once you feel that he is going to lie down, let up on the pressure on the leash. Again, make sure that you give the command "down" only once. Continue repeating this exercise until the dog lies down of his own accord on *both* the voice and hand commands. Once he lies down without your exerting any pressure on the leash, you can take off the leash and try without it. Give the voice and hand commands and praise him if he obeys. If he refuses, it means he is not quite ready for this step, so go back a step.

Remember to use as few words as possible, and isolate your basic commands. One family's dog was repeatedly found up on the furniture, even after being told to "get down" or "jump down." I handled this problem by analyzing the word "down." "Down" is a command meaning to *lie down*, not *off*. When they want their dog to get off the furniture, what they really should be saying is "no." Oddly, the owners were more upset that their dog couldn't take more sophisticated commands than they were at being unable to communicate with him. Consider how hard it is for small schoolchildren to learn the meaning of prepositions such as *in, out, through, to*. Treat your dog with the same respect.

Once he lies when *you're* standing, try it when *he's* standing. If he is proficient in following the "down" from a sitting position, as he should be by this time, then you shouldn't have too much trouble. He knows what the word means. Merely place him in a standing position and tell him to lie down. If he refuses, push him down. Continue to do this until he lies on command.

When he does this command perfectly, you are ready to link the "sit," "stay," and "down" commands together. Before doing this, however, isolate the separate commands and review any weak points.

SITTING UP FROM A LYING POSITION

A satisfied client admitted that the only thing that continued to bother him about his Weimaraner was that he had a tendency to lie down in the car. The man wanted his dog to sit straight up in the car, at attention. Unless it's your special fetish, why not let your dog be comfortable wherever he is?

Once your dog understands the "down" command thoroughly, he's ready to learn to sit back up again. Make him lie down, then give him the command to "sit," bringing your hand straight up from the "down" position. If he doesn't sit up, either jerk him up by his leash or place your foot under his chest and give him a nudge so that he is forced to sit up. Repeat this until he sits up on command. Remember always to praise him when he reaches the sitting position, no matter how he gets there, and never use too many words in a command. When a dog is lying down and you want him to sit up, use the command "sit" and not "up."

"STAND" FROM A LYING POSITION, AND "STAND" FROM A SITTING POSITION

Once he knows how to sit up from a down position, he can be taught to stand from a sit position—and even from a down position.

To get him to stand from a down position, first give the command "stand." Raise your right hand in an upward motion above your head and jerk him straight up with the leash, not allowing him to sit. As soon as he stands, give him the "stay" command and then praise him.

After he responds with only a slight jerk on the leash, take it off and try him without it. If he refuses to stand, nudge him in the ribs. This should be enough of a reminder, but if not, put his leash back on and start again. Continue practicing until he responds.

To make him stand from a sit position you follow the exact same procedure. Only this time, start him off in a sit position and make him stand from there.

By the time you've completed this training, your dog should be old enough to go outside. So when he is perfect indoors, your lessons can now proceed outdoors.

Take him out and work the exact same exercises in the exact same order that you did inside. Start him on a leash and let him work his way to freedom.

25 "Heel"

In the wild a dog can roam free and exercise himself. In the city you have to make sure he gets enough exercise by walking him and playing with him. Professional dog walkers are fine, but if you walk your dog yourself, the experience will be far more rewarding.

A six-foot leash is fine and its purpose is not only to keep your dog from running away, but also to teach him that he is to stay by your side. Every client is taught how to talk his dog properly. The dog should *walk* and not pull you down the street.

Ideally, your dog should now know enough to sit and stay when he's told to. But what's to keep him at your side when you're actually walking him? If you can't answer that one, you are in for some unpleasant experiences.

One woman's two Great Danes pulled her down the street three times a day until the dogs saw a cat on the other side of the street. A strikingly beautiful girl, who never owned even one dog bought two English setters to promenade in the park. One day both dogs headed for the same telephone pole, and each dog opted for a different side. . . .

Heeling is as important for your dog as it is for you. Which of us hasn't seen a small dog straining against his leash at a 45-degree angle, choking and gagging at his collar, his feet slipping against the pavement? And if there's too much slack in his lead, a dog can move far enough away from you and put himself right in the midst of traffic. You have to drum into your dog's head that he can't cross in front of you. When you say "sit" at a curb, your dog simply must do as you say, because some day

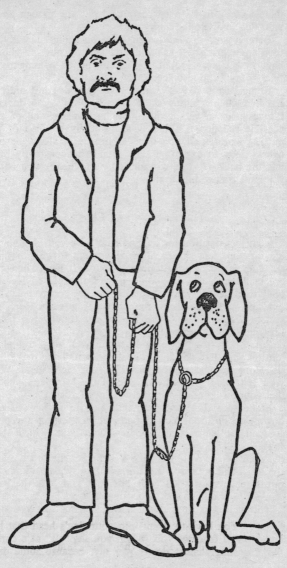

there's going to be a car coming by. Care enough about your dog to discipline him.

Before your dog learns to heel, he should already be used to wearing a leash indoors, and by now he should have had a good indoors grounding in the commands of "sit," "stay," and also "come."

Remember that you cannot take your dog out until he has had all his puppy shots. The first time you do take him out for a walk, you'll find he displays one of two possible reactions: Either he's absolutely terrified of the outside world, and you have to drag him along, or he's overanxious to explore it, and you'll be constantly pulling him back. No dog will naturally stay beside you unless you have trained him to do so.

HEELING ON THE LEASH

The correct position for heeling is to have your dog standing on your left side, and close enough to you that his shoulder is just barely touching your left leg. When you are walking him, you should almost be able to feel his body right next to your leg at all times.

Make sure you use his regular training leash. Don't invest in a chain leash. Such leashes are usually too heavy for training puppies.

Put the six-foot training leash on your dog and place him on your left side in the heel position. Then make him sit. Hold the end of the leash in your right hand. With your left hand grasp the middle of the leash and pull so that your left hand hangs freely at your left side.

Make sure that your left thumb is in a forward and downward position. You should not be exerting any pressure on the leash at all, and it should have a *little* slack to it.

When you feel comfortable about the grip you have on the leash and your dog is settling in the right position, take one step forward with your left foot and jerk the leash straight forward, giving the command "heel."

This will start your dog walking. As soon as you stop, jerk the leash straight backward saying "heel" again. This will cause your dog to stop. If he is not in the exact heel position, place him there and then praise him.

At the beginning, you must stop after each step and

jerk him into a heel position, or he will never learn it.
You must also stop every time you jerk the leash. Most
people make the mistake of walking and jerking at the
same time. The dog has no idea what you're talking about
unless you demonstrate very methodically. Take a step
and then stop, say "heel" and jerk the leash at the same
time. Remember not to *pull* on the leash, as this does
nothing. You must jerk fast and release the pressure immediately. Continue to do this step by step, jerk by jerk,
constantly using the command "heel" every step of the
way.

It's important to jerk the leash every time the dog moves
an inch out of line. One elegant woman was having great
difficulty in learning to walk her dog. "She holds the leash
like it's tissue paper," her son pointed out. It was later
learned that she didn't want to break her carefully mani-
cured fingernails.

People often don't want to jerk the leash, because they
think it hurts their dogs. Actually it doesn't hurt one bit.
It's just a way of telling your dog that you're in charge,
and he's going to follow whatever you say. There's no
need to speak to the dog, just jerk the leash. He'll get the
message if you give it to him. It will help him to stay
alive in a very dangerous, busy environment, the city.

Some people are too embarrassed to warn their dogs,
or even give them a good reprimand in front of others.
One woman was horrified at the thought of giving her
boxer "a boot in the behind" when he misbehaved outside.
"It's not ladylike at all," she complained. "Sometimes,
though, I'd like to take a club to him."

Controlling your dog in the outside world is part of dog
ownership. One Weimaraner had a problem walking with
his mistress. She was not firm enough with him and didn't
jerk on the leash properly. So the dog felt he didn't have
to toe the line and pulled her all over the place. I instructed her to establish her dominance before leaving the
house by putting her dog through some basic commands such as "sit," "stay," and "come." This worked for
her, but a proper jerk would have been easier.

It is very important that you do not turn around to your
dog. Keep walking in a straight line. If you turn to
face your dog or go off course, he will become confused
as to where he is supposed to be when heeling. The point
of this exercise is to teach him where to stand and walk in

the heel position, and that is close at your side. So, make it simple; keep both of you on one straight path until he gets some kind of idea as to what is expected of him. Also, make sure you stop at every corner and make him sit. Let him know that if anything distracting happens, you expect him to trust *you* and wait for *your* command. Jerk the leash back and say "sit." Then use your hand signal to say "stay." If you don't do this every single time you walk him, he won't sit every single time you stop. It's that simple.

One dog had a bad habit of running into traffic after his owner told him to sit at the curb. This is a situation where house keys come in handy. The dog was led right up to the curb and told to stay. If he moved, the keys were dropped in front of him. If he stayed, he was praised. Dogs do understand this small amount of pressure from their master, and the keys were only needed a few times as reinforcement.

At first you should exercise him in heeling for short intervals only (twenty-five to fifty feet). If you haven't got the time to continue working with this exercise, then don't give him the command. Once you tell him to heel, you must follow through. Even though you expect him to do it constantly when on the leash, it is a command just like all the others. So take it easy in the beginning and gradually build up the exercise until he is stopping at your side without your jerking the leash. Then start walking him and see if he will stay at your side. If he does, fine. But if he doesn't, then stop and repeat all over again until he stays at your side.

If you find that your dog pulls out in front of you, then stop short. Let him pull to the end of the leash, letting it slip out to the full six feet. Don't let go of the leash with either hand but grab hold of the end with both and jerk him hard several times saying "heel."

Make sure you jerk the leash to your left side, not toward you. One of my clients was walking his dog in the park, with a six-foot lead. When his dog moved out ahead of him, he yanked back on the leash, striking himself squarely in the groin, and fell to the ground doubled up with pain. Stand your ground and make him come back to you; don't you go to him. Once he comes back, praise him.

If he pulls out to the side, repeat the same procedure. If

he lags behind, jerk him forward in a series of short, firm jerks. If he pulls across in front of you, knee him and jerk him back, while continuously walking a straight line yourself. Never change your position for him, but make him come to you.

When you feel that he is proficient at heeling in a straight line, then you can start teaching him to heel in other directions. Eventually the jerking of the leash becomes a means of guiding him, so always jerk the leash in the direction you want him to go. This is basically quite simple once he understands the "heel" command.

After a dog can heel forward in a straight line, he can be taught to heel as you walk backward. This means that the dog has to walk backward also. The way to do this is to back up step by step, jerking the leash straight back and saying "heel" on each and every step, just as you did in teaching him to heel forward.

After a dog can do this, he should be taught to heel as in a side step, both to the left and to the right. When stepping to the right, jerk the leash to the right, and as you are stepping to the left, push him sideways with your leg. On each step say "heel." Jerk or push until he is perfect and learns to watch the direction you're moving in and to heel on command.

When making a right *turn*, give the leash a series of quick easy jerks guiding him to the right. When making a left turn, just hold the leash and come around him. Once he follows these maneuvers with ease, you can start heeling him in circles, zigzags, figure eights, and any other way you want.

Heeling perfectly on the leash means that your dog is right at your left side *at all times*. In other words, he must learn to follow your movements. Once you feel that he is perfect at heeling on the leash, then you are ready to start working without it.

HEELING OFF THE LEASH

To allow their dogs off the leash outside seems to be the ultimate hope for dog owners. Very few trainers will attempt this off-the-leash training, simply because they're afraid to take the responsibility. A trainer should be thorough enough so that the owner can trust his dog implicitly, and the dog should obey all commands.

A well-trained dog should be allowed off the leash as a reward, so that he can feel free and totally independent. If you are a nervous person and tend to panic easily, don't attempt to heel your dog off the leash except within a confined area.

Before attempting this exercise, make sure that he responds perfectly to the "come" command outside as well as indoors. He might be perfectly controllable on the leash, but many dogs will take advantage of freedom when they see it. This is why it is so important that he obey the "come" command completely and why you must work him in a confined area when he's first off the leash. Make sure he is perfect here before trying him without restrictions.

Work with him step by step, as you did when you first started to teach him the heel command. Place your dog at your left side in the heel position and, instead of jerking the leash, slap your left thigh with your left hand and give the command "heel." If he refuses to heel, then put the leash on him and heel him with the leash. After you feel he is ready, try him once more. Then, increase heeling off the leash in the same way you did heeling on the leash.

Part Four

TRICKS
AND
ADVANCED
TRAINING

26 Tricks—an Introduction

Once the chewing or biting or barking has been stopped, satisfied clients frequently decide that tricks are in order. I agree, but only after a dog has totally forgotten all his bad habits and is thoroughly housebroken and obedience-trained. I consider tricks to be a bonus.

Always make sure that your dog has a thorough basic obedience background before you attempt any tricks with him. Trick training will do no good and could be a complete frustration to you if your dog doesn't understand basic commands, since all basic commands are integrated in some way with the actual performance of any trick.

If you have already taught your dog "sit," "stay," "lie," "down," and "come," and you find any one of these commands isn't working properly, then forget everything else. Go back and work only with the command or exercise he is weak in. Do this exercise over and over until the dog responds perfectly. Only then can you go on to other commands. Always go back on any weak points you find in his basic training. Otherwise you will never be able to do more complex acts with your dog.

Most owners, naturally, are interested in having their dogs perform for their friends. The cardinal rule here is to pretend that there are no other people present. Your dog is performing for *you*, and *your* satisfaction, not your guests'. In short, concentrate on your dog, not on his audience. If he does something out of step, the dog must be corrected immediately. Some people are embarrassed when their dogs don't perform, and just laugh it off, leaving their pet to his own devices. Such a dog will never perform properly.

It is always a good idea to review his basic commands once in a while, even after he is perfect in them. After he executes all the basic commands perfectly, then start to mix the order in which you give the commands to your dog. This is to keep him aware and ready to do what you want. If you *always* tell him to sit, then lie, he is going to start anticipating. So, when you tell him to sit, he might just lie down, knowing that command comes next. On the other hand, you will want your dog to anticipate in just this fashion while teaching most of the tricks in this book. You will be linking basic commands together for greater effect, and eventually your dog *will* begin to anticipate, and will learn a routine that he will perform consistently after you give him only a single command.

When teaching a dog any advanced obedience training, hand commands are often the only way to communicate and get him to respond to you. For instance, one of the simplest but most sought-after tricks is having your dog "shake hands," that is, extend his paw when anyone makes the gesture of wanting to take it. This trick is even taught with body language, in fact. Simply tell your dog to sit and stay. Extend your hand as you would when you go to shake hands, and with your other hand gently push him to one side, throwing him slightly off balance, at the same time saying "shake hands." He will automatically lift his paw in order to regain his balance. At this point, simply take hold of his paw and shake it, saying "good boy."

By placing your hand close to the paw you want, you can get him to give you the paw of your choice on command, even to the extent of teaching him to respond to "left" or "right." But whether your friends approach him with "give me some skin," "put 'er there," or whatever, he will still understand and "shake" whenever he sees their hand coming in the appropriate gesture.

Some training manuals give hand commands that do not direct the dog but only look good. Ideally, your hand commands eventually become the trigger of any trick. For instance, in teaching a dog to jump, you constantly use the word "jump" at the time that he actually goes over the object. This way he eventually learns to associate the word with the action of jumping, but at the same time, he will also learn your accompanying gesture. At first this gesture must be very expansive, but eventually you can do it in a more contained way, so that finally a very small, even unnoticeable, gesture can be used to trigger a command.

Some animals are more attuned to visual cues than others. This does not depend on breed necessarily, but on the individual dog. If you work fairly close to any animal and coordinate your voice and hand commands with the movements of your head and eyes, eventually—by always working step by step—you should be able to get the dog to respond solely to changes in your facial expression. However, this requires much concentrated hard work.

If on television or in the movies you see a dog picking one object out of four and you can't hear his onstage trainer saying anything, he is most probably giving a head or eye command. This is total body communication between dog and trainer, and in my opinion is the greatest form of dog training.

If a dog learns to respond to the basic hand commands from the very beginning, these can eventually be linked together to form a more complex command which he will be able to perform as long as he watches your hands. Ultimately, you should be able to guide your dog by hand commands the way a conductor leads an orchestra.

Are there any limitations on the tricks which dogs can perform? It may not seem so, because your dog's ancestors have endowed him with a remarkable physical agility. I once went down the steps to a California beach, leaving Sleepy, my four-pound Maltese on the rocky cliff thirty feet above. I assumed he would use the steps too. But instead, the dog simply launched himself over the cliff in a series of short jumps from rock to rock. If he missed his footing, he still had enough stamina to leap back to his previous takeoff point, a feat generally conceded only to mountain goats.

Your dog can charge right at you and stop short, without touching you. In fact, a running dog will often brake so fast with his front feet that his hindquarters swing around into a new position, ready to launch his body in a new direction. This action is like the controlled skid employed by racing drivers.

Have you ever seen a dog and his master walking down a street where the local animals haven't been curbed? The man will usually step right in a pile, the dog never. Even when a dog's running, he's surefooted enough not to put his paws in the wrong place. Unless, of course, he doesn't *know* it's a wrong place—if, for instance, he hasn't learned to avoid the glint of a broken bottle.

Most of the time a dog will do anything for you. If something is too difficult to do, he usually just won't do it. But since he can't anticipate, he must learn by trial and error, and an eager owner can sometimes push his dog too far. When teaching your dog to do anything, check ahead of time to be sure that he is perfectly safe. There should be no surprises, otherwise you'll scare him, and he'll never trust you. Surprises have a place, but for punishments and reprimands only.

Common sense should tell you that not all dogs can do the same things. For instance, you can't expect a ten-pound dog to jump a six-foot fence. You wouldn't want to teach a dachshund to sit up on his hind legs, because his back couldn't support him. In general, Great Danes should not be taught to jump over objects. Instead of strengthening their hind legs, as it would, say, a German shepherd, the weight of the too-heavy body could damage them.

Some exercises are within a dog's capability, but are simply too complex for any but an experienced trainer to teach. One woman had seen a Lhasa do a somersault number on a television show and wanted her very own acrobatic apso. I told her that her dog could probably learn the stunt, but that I would have to teach the dog personally.

I don't attempt to teach owners to teach their dogs any complicated acrobatics that can cause physical injury to either dog or owner. I feel that the average person, no matter how well trained his dog may be, is not qualified to teach such things, because great precaution and many years of experience are required. I don't want to see any dog get hurt, so stick to the simple but effective tricks that both you and your dog can handle. Don't expect too much of your dog. Allow him his doghood. He's not meant to be an entertainer.

Some of the tricks in this book may seem almost incredibly advanced, but none of them puts your dog in the least physical danger. Nor are they the last word in dog training. They're simply a primer to show you what can be done. It's up to the individual owner to think of new stunts and try them out.

Don't try to make an animal go completely against his nature, because it is so much easier to work with what is already there. Just as each breed was bred for specific purposes, they have certain strong points and certain weaknesses, and you should take them into account. Hunting dogs are very good at any retrieving tricks, and tricks involving the sense of smell. You might use your collie or Hungarian puli to round up the children as he would sheep, for these are herding-type dogs. A water spaniel or Labrador retriever can be taught to ride on a surfing mat at the beach or dive down under water to retrieve clams from the bottom.

Use your common sense along with your imagination and think up little tricks for your dog to learn in accordance with his breed and background.

27 "Roll Over" and "Play Dead"

Many times I have to convince my clients that exercising the dog in obedience is the best way to get him to perform well. One lady got her dog to roll over by using a hair dryer on him. I explained that she could have had him do the same thing without props, after some constant coaxing and practice.

When teaching your dog to roll over, you must remember that he doesn't really like to do this. It tends to throw him off balance, and an animal likes to be in complete control of his body at all times. Rolling over is not harmful in any way, however, and *is* a cute trick.

This is one of the few tricks for which I use a treat in training the dog. First make your dog lie down, then take a dog biscuit and tempt him with it, while holding him in a lying position. When he starts to get interested in it, pass it in a circular motion over his shoulders and around his back very slowly, keeping it just out of reach of his mouth.

His nose will follow the biscuit like a donkey after a carrot. His head cannot go around in a complete circle, and so he has to move his body around with his head in order to follow the movement of the biscuit. In this way, he will naturally have to roll over, and while he is doing so, use the command "roll over."

After he rolls over completely, praise him and give him the biscuit. Repeat this exercise over and over, switching sides occasionally until he understands. After you feel confident that he does understand, back away a little and try making the motion—with the biscuit in your hand—from a distance. If he does it, increase your distance. If not, go back to the stage that he completed properly and work ahead from there. Eventually, of course, you will no longer be using a biscuit to tempt your dog. The circular motion made by your hand will become the hand command for this trick. Ultimately, you should be able to make a circular motion with one hand, and your dog, wherever he is, should lie down and roll over. But even if you don't want to get quite this sophisticated, do keep working until he does this trick to your satisfaction.

PLAY DEAD

The same roll-over technique is used to teach your dog to play dead while lying on his back. The way to do this is to have him roll over, then stop him when he reaches the point where he has rolled onto his back. Quickly give the command "stay," which he should have mastered in his basic training. Hold him there until you want to release him from the trick, then give him your release word such as "okay." After you release him, praise him thoroughly and give him the biscuit.

Please always remember that "good boy" is not a release word, it is praise. A dog should always have a word which releases him from all of his commands, and he should know even from the first day of training what this word is. So pick the word you want at the very beginning and use it consistently.

Remember to use hand commands with all verbal commands from the very beginning also: for "play dead," a semicircular motion followed by a sharp stay motion will be the command.

Obviously, the "roll over" should be learned before the "play dead," as this makes the latter exercise much easier for him.

28 Jumping—Over and Through

Jumping is not only a good-looking and exciting trick, but also an extremely practical one—especially if you don't live in the country. In the city there is very little space and opportunity for a dog to exercise, and this situation shows no sign of improvement. Jumping condenses a dog's running into a compact controlled exercise, and is one way of making up for the ten-mile walk per day that is advisable for larger dogs.

For example, Labrador retrievers are strong sporting dogs, built low in their hindquarters. Many aging Labs have trouble getting about, simply because their hind leg muscles weaken with age (as do most dogs' legs). But if Labradors are trained to jump as puppies, their hind legs can be strengthened enough to avoid later deterioration. It's simply a matter of exercise, training those hind legs into proportion with the rest of the body. This fact holds true for all breeds.

Before starting on jumping, however, make sure the dog is physically fit to do so. Check with your vet and have him pay special attention to the dog's hind legs. I don't recommend teaching some dogs of particular breeds—such as Great Danes, St. Bernards, Newfoundlands, Great Pyrenees, Irish wolfhounds or mastiffs—to jump, because if these dogs have hind-leg problems, the jumping could do them damage. Only jump dogs, and especially these breeds, with a veterinarian's approval.

Four to six months is about the best time to start training your dog to jump. Before this time, his hind legs are not developed enough to support a jump, and he could possibly injure himself. Nor should you teach your dog to

jump until after he has been thoroughly basic obedience-trained and knows such commands as "sit," "stay," and "come." A great deal of control is necessary before you can accomplish this trick, but if you have started obedience training at about six weeks of age—which is my recommendation—your dog should be very well behaved by the age of four to six months. Thorough obedience-training is necessary before *any* of the more complex tricks are taught. Moreover, the more tricks you can teach a dog while he's young, the more they will be second nature to him when he grows up.

When you start teaching your dog to jump, get yourself a hurdle that's not too high—say twelve inches for large dogs and half that for small dogs. It should be no trouble to nail a few old boards together, but whatever you decide to use as the hurdle, make sure it can be fastened securely to the ground, floor, or wall. Indoors, I recommend placing it securely in the doorway between two rooms. The reason for this is that if your dog accidentally knocks it over, he might never want to try jumping again. By the same token, I suggest covering the board with a towel or a blanket because if he hits a hard surface, it could hurt him. Remember that once hurt, a dog will become frightened and never forget, so be very careful the first few times until he gains confidence. This same principle holds true for any new trick, including any jumps over tricky or unusual objects.

Now that you are all set up, put a six-foot training leash on your dog and bring him to one side of the hurdle. Use no commands, not even "sit" or "stay." Step over to the other side of the board still holding the leash. Now pull your dog toward you.

Chances are he won't follow you on his own because the object is new to him, and he is cautious. But simply pull him coaxingly over the hurdle, saying "jump." Use no other word but "jump" as he is being pulled over. With this, as with all other commands, make sure that the dog completes the exercise every time you give the command. If he can't or won't jump, nudge or pull him over. If he gets away with not doing it once, he'll try not doing it again and again.

When he gets over the obstacle, no matter how reluctantly, praise him profusely. Then step over to the other side of the board and repeat the whole thing. Remember that praise is very important in this trick, as it is in all tricks. Dogs live to please you, and your approval encourages them.

Work for only five minutes at a time with lots of rest in between exercises. Otherwise he'll get bored and won't see jumping as the thrilling, exhilarating stunt it ought to be.

Repeat this exercise until the dog comes over to your side of the hurdle without any pulling of the leash. Then take the leash off him and make him jump over to you. If you find him a little obstinate once the leash is off, call him to you. But just as he reaches the hurdle, use the word "jump." And as he completes the jump, give him plenty of praise. You are praising him for jumping, not for coming to you.

If this still doesn't work, go back a step and put the leash on him. Whenever things aren't going right, go back to the stage where your dog *was* doing the right thing!

Once he can jump on command without a leash over this small hurdle, put the leash back on him. Make him sit and stay close to the hurdle, with you on the *same* side this time. Point over it with one hand and hold the leash in the other, telling your dog to "jump." If he balks, jerk the leash. As soon as he starts to go over, *drop* the leash. When he has gone over, then step over the hurdle to him, praise him, and repeat the exercise from that side of the hurdle.

Take the leash off once he obeys without your having to jerk on it. By now he should be able to jump whenever you point your finger and give the command. If he doesn't, go back to the stage he can do and start from there. At this point he should have enough confidence so that you can remove the towel from his hurdle. It is also the right time for you to start putting the hurdle in different spots around the house or yard. Gradually move back from the hurdle, so that your dog has to run a distance to reach it before jumping.

If he does all this well, you can try changing the object he is to jump. If you don't vary the position and type of obstacle, you may find that your dog will refuse to jump anything but the original hurdle. One of my friends taught his dog to jump a small fence on New York's 36th Street. He and his dog have since moved to Connecticut, but whenever he wants to prove that his dog can jump, he has to come back to the city to do it. So please use variety. But each and every time you change to a new obstacle, start him off on a leash again. This will make sure that the dog knows that you are asking him to jump.

Once your dog is bounding over whatever you point to (as long as it's within his reach), then you can proceed to teach him trick jumping such as through a hoop. Most owners don't realize that the concept of jumping *through* a hoop is simply not a natural act for an animal.

Originally your pet cleared the hurdle because it was set up in a doorway and the only way for him to get "around" it was in a vertical direction. He thus learned the concept of *up and over,* but if I ask my dog to jump a vertical object like a garbage can and he thinks it's a bit too high for him, he will jump, but slightly to one side of the can, just to protect himself. An animal is used to going to one side, or under, or over obstacles, and sees no point in going *through* them unless the aperture is like a doorway, enclosed on all sides. To be able to jump through a hoop, he must learn to go *over* the bottom, *under* the top, and *between* the two sides, which is slightly more complex than a simple flying leap.

Take a large hula hoop, wrap it all around with toweling, and set up the original hurdle you used when you first started to teach your dog to jump. Put the leash on your dog and place him on one side of the hurdle. Then feed the end of the leash through the hoop and place yourself on the opposite side of the hurdle, holding the leash with one hand and the hoop steady on top of the hurdle with the other. Then giving the command "jump," pull your dog over the hurdle and through the hoop. Continue in the same way you did when first teaching your dog to jump *over.* Once he gets the idea, remove the hurdle and hope for the best.

Again, don't forget this is not a natural act for a dog, so use a great deal of patience and plenty of praise. It may help if there's another dog around who can perform the trick perfectly. Then your dog is likely to pick up the concept and do it properly. But conversely, don't train more than one dog at a time, since the results can be disastrous when each dog picks up the mistakes of his fellow pupil.

I once tried to show a friend that my dogs were trained to jump *through* things. I took a large, roughly circular wire sculpture down off its pedestal and placed it, neatly blocking a doorway, then told my dogs to jump through the central aperture.

This should have worked, except that the first small Maltese, who came to the doorway first, had never jumped through this particular apparatus before. So instead of risking a jump and possibly getting hurt, he simply evaded the issue—ducked his head and squeezed under the sculpture's lower hoop. The other Malteses followed suit. My Weimaraner, following after them, naturally tried to go under it himself, but not being built so close to the ground, he only succeeded in shouldering the sculpture off balance. It capsized with a terrible clatter, and he had to scramble frantically to get out of the way. The piece wasn't damaged, but it became more difficult for me to teach him to jump *through* that particular sculpture, since his first try ended in racket and embarrassment.

29 "Out" or "Go"

Certain exercises such as jumping, fetching, and tracking are directed from a distance. If the command "out" or "go" is taught correctly, you can send your dog out in any direction you want, merely by pointing in that direction—and when he gets there, you can give him any other commands you want. He should, of course, respond immediately to these other commands, for at this point in his training you should already have taught your dog all the very basic commands, and he should really enjoy doing them to please you. At the same time, the "out" or "go" command is a means of getting your dog used to moving in whatever direction your hand points.

You can also use this command, of course, when you simply don't want your dog around—but be careful. Many people have a tendency to use it as a reprimand, like sending a child to bed without supper. This technique does not work with dogs any better than it does with children. In fact, it has even less effect with a dog, because he does not understand what you are trying to do.

Many people make the related error of saying "go away" or "get out of here" when their dog has done something wrong. This is a very bad mistake, as the dog may never learn the "go" or "out" command correctly once it has been used as a punishment. I don't say to be *nice* to your dog after he has done something wrong. I mean that you should reprimand him immediately and then ignore him, but never send him from you as a punishment.

To make your dog understand the word "out" or "go," whichever you prefer or the obedience trails demand, start teaching your dog indoors, where you can control his movements. First put a leash on your dog and walk him over to a doorway. Then gently push or pull his leash until he crosses over the threshold into the other room, but don't cross over yourself. At the same time, give the command "out" or "go," pointing with one hand. When he gets there, tell him "stay," go to him and praise him very enthusiastically. Passing from one room to another gives him a very definite objective, and he can easily associate the word with crossing the threshold. You must show excitement in your praise because your dog has learned to be secure in your company—so when first doing this, he may think you are sending him away because you are displeased with him, and sulk out of the room. If you praise him with great gusto, he will quickly get the idea that it is a good thing to do.

Continue this exercise till the dog seems to be going through the doorway on his own or with very little help. Then go on to the next step. Take off the leash. Sit him facing the open doorway. Stand on his right side and point to the doorway, giving the command "out" or "go." If he does it properly, go to him and praise him, then repeat this exercise going in the opposite direction through the doorway. If he doesn't respond, nudge him through, and praise him when he's completed it.

Continue this exercise, gradually increasing your mutual distance from the doorway. But do not try to increase the distance until he is completely ready. If he fails to respond properly at any point, then go back a step until he is responding perfectly to both voice and hand commands. Remember to say "out" only *once*. If he refuses to respond to your command, you must *make* him do so. Start walking into him, pushing him out. You must stop the instant he starts going on his own, and praise him when he does the right thing, which in this case is when he gets through the doorway.

Once he seems to have this down pat, then take him to other rooms and do the same exercise. This will get him accustomed to working in different areas. Always remember to start working with your dog at a very close distance to the doorway, and as he learns the command, gradually increase the distance.

Keep in mind that one of the objects of this command is to make your dog look to you for direction at all times. Wouldn't you feel funny if you were pointing in one direction and he ran the opposite way? So after he starts responding to "go" with some ease, change the direction. Don't always have him facing in the direction you want him to go, sometimes turn his back to the doorway and then point to it to make sure that he is following your hand directions. Even face him toward one door and point to another.

If he starts off in the wrong direction, quickly use the word "no." When he stops, call him. When he gets to you, don't praise him, but make him sit. Start all over and gently push him in the right direction. He should be praised only for completing the command correctly. Go through this process very gradually and use patience. Once he gets accustomed to watching your hand, you will be able to control the direction he moves in.

When he is perfect inside, then you are ready to work him outside. Remember, this command should be taught only after all the basic obedience commands so that you can safely work with him outside, knowing that he will come back when you call him. Otherwise, his response to the command of "go" may well turn out to be permanent.

Before going ahead to new locations, always go back a step to make sure he knows the command. As with all the other exercises, work with him for short intervals.

Don't tempt him to "go" by planting a bone or toy. I only use these to start teaching him tracking or complete direction finding, so I wait till he has learned the "out" or "go" command 100 percent perfectly. If and when he gets this, *then* you can place two of his favorite toys, such as a ball and a bone, in one room. Then point in the direction of one of the objects, telling your dog "go." When he starts to go, then say "go get the ball" or "go get the bone," whichever you are pointing toward. When he gets the correct object, praise him. If he doesn't do it properly, repeat till he does. When he does all of this perfectly, take the objects away and start sending him out in various directions merely by pointing. After he starts following your hand directions, you can then start sending him out to jump, fetch, or just to sit or lie somewhere.

30 Carrying and Retrieving

All of these exercises are concerned with a dog's natural instinct to catch and carry objects in his mouth, plus his ability to respond to "body language" in the form of hand commands.

A good rule in training is to start with the hardest problem first, not the most complex, but the hardest for your dog to understand. As any owner of a chewing dog will tell you, what a dog likes to hold in his mouth is not necessarily the item you'd like him to. For this simple reason, you must teach your dog to carry the object of *your* choice.

Before starting out to train a dog to fetch or carry, he must understand that he is supposed to *hold* the required object in his mouth *only,* not chew it. To get this crucial concept across, you must first teach him to hold and drop on command.

The key to this exercise is the command "stay." First make the dog sit and stay. Take the object you want your dog to retrieve and gently place it in his mouth. Make sure that whatever you want him to carry cannot harm him in any way. If he refuses to accept it, then place your hand over his muzzle and press your thumb and forefinger inward, putting pressure on his jowls right behind the canines, known in the movies as "fangs." His mouth will automatically open. After his mouth is open, place the object into it saying "take it," and close his mouth around the object by holding his jaws shut with your hand. Quickly push the palm of your other hand near his nose in a definite, emphatic "stay" motion, but using the verbal command "hold it," instead. At the same time you say this,

187

let go of his muzzle and back up one step, with your hand remaining in the "stay" position.

As soon as he starts to chew or let it drop (as he usually will at first), say "no," and hold his muzzle shut. If he holds it, which is very unlikely the first few times, keep your hand in the stay position and praise him continuously. Do not use the release word, or you will ruin everything. If he drops it, patiently go through the process over and over until he eventually catches on. The most important thing for you to remember is not to lose your temper or become disgusted, or you won't be able to teach him anything. He will learn, but only by patient repetition. When he starts to hold the object, gradually increase the length of time he is to hold on to it.

After he can hold an object on command for a minute or more, you can teach him how to "drop it." To get him to drop the object, you simply put your hand below his mouth ready to catch it. Your hand held in a palm-upward position, as if ready to catch the object, will serve as the hand signal in the future. If he doesn't drop it right off, with the other hand repeat the process used to make him open his mouth, this time also using the verbal command "drop it." Repeat this until he drops the object on command, with no assistance. Eventually, the hand command alone will be enough to make him drop it, but as you practice this exercise, remember to back further away gradually, since you will not want to have to stick your hand under his mouth every time you want him to drop something.

Once he can do this, he can carry your newspaper, slippers, bag, or whatever you want, which is certainly one of the favorite tricks. Two words of reservation however: he is not yet ready to be trusted with a package from the butcher shop, unless you have taught him to take, hold, drop—and not chew—something that is blatantly edible, such as a dog biscuit; also, remember that no dog has a completely dry mouth. The presence of an object in his mouth will automatically cause some secretion of saliva, so don't ask him to carry any suede shoes, or articles that could be damaged by more than an iota of slobber.

Once your dog has mastered the hold-and-drop exercise, he is ready for controlled retrieving. You can now control him to the point where he will hold any object of your choice on command, sit and stay until you release him, and drop it when you tell him to. The problem is to teach him to get the object at a distance and bring it back to you. In order to do this he must first have learned the command "out" or "go," which we explained earlier, so that your dog will run in whatever direction you point.

This, again, is a good example of the importance of a dog's understanding hand commands. If he knows how to follow the motion of your hand, he knows the direction you want him to go. If not, you should go back to basic training and either teach or review your hand commands, because as I said before, even in the best trained dogs, including mine, constant reminder and repetition is the only way to retain perfection. A dog will always try to test you and dominate. This is his nature, and you must constantly prove you are the dominant leader.

If you want your dog to retrieve, a much simpler one-word command is "fetch." But this command is also the first of the "compound" commands which we promised you earlier composed of "out" or "go," "take it," "hold it," "sit/stay," and finally "drop it." To teach him to fetch properly, you must run through these commands in sequence after saying "fetch," until he associates the whole string with the initial, single command.

Your first step is to tempt him with the object. After he is really interested in it, throw it out a short distance. He will usually go after it. If he does, use the word "out" or "fetch" or even your own command as long as it doesn't interfere with any other commands he's learned. Don't say it too loudly, because he might think you are reprimanding him and not go out after the object.

If he goes out and picks up the object, tell him to "hold it." Call him to you with the word "come." When he gets to you, tell him to "drop it," and when he does so, praise him.

Repeat this exercise until it becomes second nature to him. However, if he breaks down anywhere along the line (for instance, if he goes out after the object but refuses to take it in his mouth and bring it back), isolate the command he has trouble with (in this example, "take it") and review it until he's perfect. Each of these commands has already been explained, and any that he doesn't know perfectly, please review. In fact, put him through each command on an isolated basis, just to be sure. Sometimes even I have to remember that a dog, no matter how well-trained, will still have his own prejudices and preferences. One day at the beach, I was having a great time throwing a football around, and wanted to get my dog to fetch it back to me. But a football is not built to fit in the mouth of an average-sized dog. After trying to pick it up, Plum got frustrated and gave up. Now, for dog owners who complain of their own pet's reluctance to fetch, I tell them to throw something their dogs can and will handle.

Once your dog performs retrieving perfectly, you are ready to practice variations on the basic exercise. These could include "lie down" and "stay" once he actually picks up the object, and coming only after you call him, jumping hurdles and *then* retrieving or vice versa, and anything else he knows how to do, even rolling over once he has retrieved. This is why I emphasize knowing each command thoroughly, because every real "trick" is based on chaining basic commands. A child cannot learn to ride a bike without learning a series of specific motions, and the same thing is true for dogs. Once these are thoroughly known, by both voice and hand commands, then your imagination and your dog's physical abilities are your only limitations.

Remember that a dog can learn between eighty and a hundred commands in his lifetime, so take advantage of it. Don't hesitate to teach him routines comprised of any or all of his basic commands.

31 Fetching by Scent Discrimination

For one of my favorite tricks, I have Plum sit and stay, then I walk off about ten paces and put a five-dollar and a ten-dollar bill on the floor, about a foot apart from each other. Plum then goes and fetches whichever bill I tell him to. This is a fairly simple example of a chained command, evolving from both the "fetch" command and the "shake hands" trick discussed earlier.

I initially taught Plum to shake hands, then to distinguish left from right merely by saying, give me your left paw, or right paw, as the case might be. Along with the verbal command I, of course, used a hand signal, pointing to the paw I wanted. Plum now understands the difference between left and right, but if your dog doesn't as yet, you can probably make it appear as if he does through careful use of hand signals.

Once Plum understood the difference between left and right, I extended this lesson to placing two objects a few feet in front of me and then pointing to the left one, at the same time saying "fetch left," or pointing to the right and saying "fetch right."

After a while Plum learned to pick the correct one by following both voice and hand commands. I then eliminated the voice command and merely used the hand command. Once Plum responded to this, I gradually made my hand commands less and less noticeable. Eventually I merely had to make a slight motion with either hand, and Plum knew what was expected of him.

At the same time, I varied the objects I expected Plum to retrieve. It took a great deal of time and patience but was well worth the effort. Sometimes people want to make things more complicated. They try to trip me up by asking me to have my dog retrieve a specific object from among several. In this case I can't use my normal signal, and so I make sure I get a chance to hold the object to be retrieved in my hand—"Oh, do you mean this one?"—so that my odor is on it before it's put down on the floor. Then I send Plum out to get it.

He usually hesitates for a while, waiting for my signal, but I cannot give any hand commands at all, only the verbal command of "fetch it." My personal smell is now his only clue. He wants to please me and, with no other clue to go on, uses his most highly developed sense. Most times he does this with ease, but unfortunately I cannot always help any slight but involuntary motions with my hand, so sometimes he makes a mistake and picks the wrong thing.

I have a way to save the situation, however, because besides everything else, Plum knows enough to look at me for my approval, which just shows the importance of praising your dog for doing the right thing. If I show any sign of disapproval, such as a frown, Plum drops what he's carrying and goes back again. This time he knows it's the odor he must look for and picks the right one. When he is right, I always give him some signal such as a smile or a quick "good boy" so that he has no chance of being confused. People are always fascinated and try to see what signal I give, but it is so subtle they usually cannot.

I also have a trick where my dog picks the correct magazine from a choice of several. In this case I don't have to use any kind of signal, since he has learned to distinguish some of the more popular magazines such as *Vogue, TV Guide,* and *New York Magazine,* using the size differences and cover patterns as his clue. In other words, he has learned to associate the name with a magazine of a particular size. This has taken years to accomplish and is no longer a "trick," but a feat of memory and reasoning on his part.

If you want to teach your dog to do either of these two tricks, he must first of all have completely mastered the retrieving exercise, by responding to both hand and voice. Once he has done this and is proficient in retrieving, he is ready to learn an intermediate step—how to retrieve merely by using his sense of smell.

It is best to start with something he is used to, but

preferably not a ball, since a ball tends to roll when
nudged or sniffed at, and this motion can easily distract
him. The best substitute is one of the plain wooden dumbbells used in obedience trials. They are easy for a dog to
pick up and carry, since his mouth can close completely
around them.

Keep throwing the dumbbell out and getting him to
bring it back as if it were second nature to him, just as
you did with his toys when you first started teaching him
to retrieve. After he's used to it, have someone place two
identical dumbbells about ten feet to one side of where
the dumbbell you throw usually lands. The whole point,
of course, is that these two should *not* have your smell on
them.

Remember that to teach scent discrimination, you must
make sure that only one object has your scent on it. That
is why it is important that someone else place the other
dumbbells. You must never even touch them, since they
will then be tainted with your odor, and he won't know
what to do. If you cannot get anyone to place them for
you, then use a shovel or kitchen tongs. Never use gloves,
for they have your odor on them, and the slightest touch
of anything that smells of you can destroy everything.

Gradually throw—or simply place—the dumbbell he
retrieves with ease closer and closer to the other odorless
dumbbells. Work at this for five to ten minutes, and stop
for about half an hour or so to let both you and your dog
rest. If he gets tired or bored, he won't want to retrieve
any dumbbell. Moreover, if you are working him outdoors
in the summer, make sure that you do so early in the
morning or in the early evening. Never work in the hot
sun, because it could do your dog harm. The only tricks
to do at this time of day are water tricks.

Keep throwing or placing your dumbbell closer and
closer to the others until eventually it is right next to them.
Your dog should automatically pick out the familiar one,
and if so, the trick is done! If he takes the wrong one, tell
him "no" and make him drop it, as he has been taught.
Go back to throwing or placing it at a distance from the
others, and gradually bring it closer again.

To make your dog perform properly, make sure *you*
know what you're doing. One of my clients complained
to me that his dog could not do this trick no matter how
hard and long he worked on it, so I went over to check on

exactly what he was doing. When I got there, he proceeded to demonstrate. He threw a dumbbell out as far as he could in one direction, and when the dog took off after it, he quickly and daintily picked up two other dumbbells, one in each hand by the thumb and forefinger, and ran on tiptoe very quietly in the opposite direction. He then dropped them quickly and ran back to his original position. When I asked him what on earth he was doing, he explained that this was where his dog broke down. He kept on hiding these two other dumbbells with his scent on them, but his dog couldn't find them at all. I had to explain that no dog is going to keep sniffing around after he's already fetched one object and that, moreover, this trick is an exercise in scent discrimination, not a scavenger hunt. The fact that he had missed the point of the exercise completely didn't surprise me as much as the fantastic speed with which the owner executed this whole procedure.

After your dog can handle one dumbbell out of three, you can start to use different objects. Either have him pick the correct object from among several identical ones, or from a variety of different objects. But when working with a number of identical objects, remember to mark the correct one so you can be sure that he retrieved it. Your sense of smell isn't as keen as his.

32   Shopping

The ultimate in fetching stunts is Plum's feat of shopping
for his own dog food in my absence, as was mentioned in
the first chapter. Again, this is the result of a long series
of separate tricks that were eventually chained together
to form one. The best way to explain this trick is to tell
you how I taught my dog to do it. I cannot give you exact
directions, since I don't know what the shopping situation
is like in your neighborhood. I think that by changing a
few particulars, you can probably teach your own dog to
shop. The first thing I did was to take Plum over to the
dog-food shelves in the local supermarket—with the manager's permission, of course. I would bring a piece of dog
candy, put it on the shelf just a few inches from the edge,
and then let Plum take it and eat it. I did this until, whenever we went into the supermarket, Plum would go straight
to the dog-food shelf to get his candy.

Once this was a well-established pattern of behavior,
I had one of the store assistants place the treat on the
shelf for me. This way Plum no longer waited for me to
put it there.

The next step was to make him sit in front of the shelf
and not allow him to take the candy, which had already
been placed there before our arrival. Instead, I would
place two cans just in front of the candy, making sure
he could see that it was still there. I would then tell him
to get his treat, and to do so he had to take it from behind
the cans. Once we established this, I proceeded to place
a bunch of cans on either side of the original two, leaving
just enough space for Plum to insert his nose. However,
the space was just small enough that in order actually to

pick up the candy, Plum would have to knock the two cans in front of it off the shelf.

I kept at this until he went straight for the shelf, didn't even bother to sniff, but simply knocked off those two cans. Needless to say, the candy was always there, not to disappoint him.

I then started on another step involving the commands, "take it," "hold it," and "drop it," all of which your dog should know by now. Whenever I went into the supermarket, I made Plum pick up or "take" one of the small carry-around shopping baskets that most stores have in addition to carts. I then heeled him to the dog-food shelf, making him hold the basket in his mouth all the way. When we got over to the shelf, I sat him down with the basket in his mouth, directly in front of the two cans hiding his treat. I then gave him the command to "drop it." He simply dropped the basket to the ground, directly in front of the cans. Then I told him to get his treat, which he did, and by doing so, knocked the cans into the basket. After he ate his candy, I told him to pick up or "take"

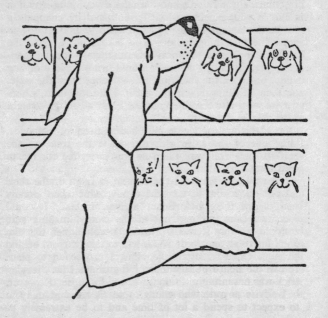

the basket, "hold it," and then "heel," until we got to the counter.

Prior to doing this I had made arrangements with the checkout girl to take Plum's basket and give him a cookie in return, so that he was rewarded for handing his basket over to the clerk. I made him sit and stay. She put the cans in a bag, and when she handed it back to him, I gave him the command to "take it." I then heeled him back out of the store and around the corner to my house.

I repeated this process over and over for about two months, and only then did I feel confident enough to let him try it alone. Well, he bombed out. So I had to go back and start again, only this time I gradually gave him his freedom in the store. I made sure that he picked up the basket, but rather than heel him to the shelf, I allowed him to go there by himself. After he did this, I made sure that my helper in the store had *not* set any treat behind the cans and I stood back by the front counter to see what would happen. He ran to the shelf, dropped the basket in front of it, and knocked the cans down, looking for his treat. When he couldn't find it, I immediately called him to "take" the basket and come to me at the counter where I had the girl give him a treat.

I continued this procedure, switching the treats around. One day they were behind the cans, and the other they weren't. He always had a fifty-fifty chance of getting one, so he naturally always took a quick look to see if it was there. But no matter what, the girl at the counter always had a treat for him. This way, he wouldn't hang around the dog-food shelves knocking down cans right and left, because he had learned the girl at the counter had a reward for him even if the cans didn't. On the other hand, he wasn't sure there *wasn't* some candy behind the cans, so rather than just head back to the counter for one certain reward, he always tried for two. After about another month of working it became a routine for him.

I then offered to let a dog-food company film Plum going into the grocery store for his shopping routine. However, the dog-food company's advertising manager felt that dogs shouldn't be allowed in supermarkets and threatened to call the Board of Health on the grounds that the whole trick was unsanitary.

I advise anyone who wants to teach his dog this trick to expect to spend a lot of time and to be extremely patient. Don't forget that if he goes wrong on any aspect, you should work on that weak point until perfect. This is the same advice I give on *all* tricks, but then, why should it be any different? The trick, and the training, may be difficult, but the principles are always the same.

33 Diving and Surfing

Water tricks are ideal exercises for when you're at the beach or in the country, especially in the heat of summer, when any other exercise would leave your dog panting and uncomfortable. It makes sense, though, to teach water tricks only to dogs who are naturally good swimmers and who really enjoy water. I say *dogs* who enjoy water, not *breeds,* because I cannot really specify any breed as being better for this type of trick than any other, for I have seen dogs of every conceivable breed and mixture who love water. One mixed breed—half Labrador, and half boxer—used to enjoy plunging into Long Island Sound and swimming after the seagulls that flew overhead. He didn't really have much expectation of catching them. He simply liked the exercise—so much that he even went in for dips in January. However, there are certain breeds who were created specifically to be water dogs: the American and Irish water spaniels; English and Welsh springer spaniels; golden retrievers; yellow and black Labrador retrievers; flat-coated, curly-coated, and Chesapeake Bay retrievers; poodles; Newfoundlands; and otterhounds, to name a few.

Once your dog can retrieve on command and can also swim, there is absolutely no reason why you can't make him retrieve a stick or ball which you throw into the water. But for a dog who likes swimming, water-retrieving is absolute puppy's play. Diving down under water to retrieve an object from the bottom is only one of the tricks that can be taught to water-loving dogs.

DIVING

You'll notice that when dogs swim, they normally keep their heads way out of the water, partly because they don't like to get water in their ears. Some dogs will briefly put their noses under water and blow bubbles, almost experimentally, but the most difficult trick to teach a dog is how to submerge his whole head under water. I suggest working in calm shallow water when starting on this feat. A lake with a graded bottom or a pool with steps are good places to begin.

In teaching a dog to dive, I use clams as the objects to be fetched. Waterlogged wood and stones have no odor. But clams have a tangy, meaty smell about them that makes them far more appealing. You may have to open a couple of clams for your dog before he gets the idea there's really anything to them, but once your dog has zeroed in on clams, it's a cinch to have him help you dig a pail of them for supper.

Tempt your dog with a clam, throw it for him on dry land, and have him bring it back to you a few times. Then take him to the lake's edge or the first step of the pool. Don't throw the clam in, but hold it in your hand under his nose. Gently lower it just below the surface of the water and out of reach of his mouth. Tell him to "take it." If he refuses to take it, then bring it up to the level where he will take it, and when he does, praise him. If he likes the taste, you can even open the clam for him as a reward. Repeat this procedure over and over, gradually lowering the clam further and further under the water's surface. Make sure the dog takes the clam each time before lowering it any further in the water. The early stages of this trick are the most difficult, as he has to learn to submerge first his nose, then his eyes, then his ears and finally his whole head under water—and dogs don't like this.

Once you get him to submerge his head, then it is just a matter of patience and work to get the rest of your dog's body to follow and have him retrieving objects from the bottom. Don't expect miracles in this particular trick. It is not something that is suddenly going to click. Careful, slow, patient work at every step of the way is necessary. Five-minute intervals is more than sufficient time to work in.

Once you have achieved retrieving from the bottom right in front of his nose, you can start to work at throwing the clam and sending him to retrieve after it sinks. The dog paddle is not the most efficient means of underwater propulsion, so throw it no more than a few inches further at each stage of training. And remember that the depth a dog can reach is proportional to his size. Don't ask a toy poodle to dive six feet.

SURFING

In ten weeks on Fire Island, I taught Plum to surf in the ocean. The reactions of bystanders are varied. Some are shocked at the thought that a dog can do such things. Others are sure it's a gimmick: Aren't his legs taped to the raft?

No, they're not. Plum takes the mat in his mouth and swims out through the surf, climbs aboard, and rides the waves back to shore, even when I am not in the water with him.

This trick does take a lot of time and patience. Again, it is best to start off in a pool or lake.

The first thing to do is to get him to enjoy being on a mat. Use an air mattress. Your dog's feet cannot get a grip on the smooth, polished surface of a regular surfboard. Put on his collar, then wade out waist deep, carrying your mat with you, and call your dog. If he enjoys swimming, as he must if you hope to teach him this trick, he will gladly come out to you.

The reason why you have gone out to waist level is so that your dog's legs can no longer touch bottom. You and the mat, rather than the solid ground under his feet, will give him his sense of security. After he reaches you, grab hold of his collar. Ease him onto the raft in a playful but firm manner. If you force or fight with him, you will blow the trick before you even start.

Remember too that your dog cannot tread water efficiently, and must circle to stay afloat, so don't try to hold him still in the water. Moreover, his natural buoyancy will decrease as he comes out of the water, so be careful you don't choke him. It's a great help to have someone else beside you to hold the raft steady, since manipulating a wet dog the size of a Weimaraner plus a bobbing, unattached raft, in two and a half feet of water, is no picnic.

When he finally is on the raft, pull him around in the water *very* gently so that he can get used to this new feeling. The main reason why he must be treated with such care is that it is so complicated for him to learn to balance himself, and doing water tricks is basically against all the natural instincts of a land animal. Until he has time to adjust, being on the raft gives him a feeling of helplessness. Surely you remember how you felt when you first tried to get into a rowboat or canoe? It usually takes quite a few times on the raft before the dog learns to balance himself, so do expect to spend a lot of time on this stage if you want him to do this trick correctly.

Once you feel that he is *completely* happy and comfortably balanced on the raft, then you can proceed. I cannot judge at what point this will happen, and therefore I must leave it up to your better judgment. I know you want only the best for your dog, and would not want to push him to the point of being hurt. Remember, all the basic training for this trick must be done in calm, placid water with you right there to assist. As with all other tricks, never go beyond the stage that he can perform properly. Go back and back again until he's perfect, and practice for very short intervals at a time.

When you feel he's ready, start to give him simple, compact exercises to do while on the raft, such as sitting, staying, lying down, and sitting back up. If he is to be able to surf, he must learn to have complete confidence and control of himself on the raft.

After he learns this, gradually back away from the raft and give him the commands of "sit," "stay," etc. Always make sure that you have a line attached to the raft so it can't drift away from you. After he can respond to commands from a distance, get behind him and start pushing the raft from the rear, so that he gets used to the feeling of floating free without you there for reassurance. These are the last phases of training that will take place in the lake or pool. When all this is accomplished, and believe me, it is a lot of patient hard work on your part, it is time to shift to the ocean.

The first time you try him in the surf, make sure it is a very calm day. Again take the raft out waist deep and call your dog out to you. Put him up on the raft, giving him no commands except "stay." Get behind the raft and gently shove it to shore.

If he jumps off halfway in, start all over and do it again. Your job is to make sure that he catches the right wave. He can't decide for himself that every third, fourth or fifth wave is the right one.

You should be able to judge how much work he can take. Never overwork him. After the first time out, you can start increasing the size of the waves that you want him to ride on. Make this a very gradual change, because this is one trick that can be completely destroyed by one mistake.

When he "wipes out," as he eventually will, you must restore as much of his confidence as possible. Pull him out of the water as quickly as you can, praise him, put him back on the raft immediately, praise him again, then pull him in to shore. (This is the same principle as getting right back on a horse after you've fallen off.) The next day, if the ocean is calm, take him back out and again work him through the basic steps of this trick, up to the point of actual surfing. See at what point he gets uneasy, and then go back a step and start to build up again from there. If you follow this procedure every time he wipes out or falls off, eventually he will get used to falling off and become a top surfer.

One word of caution: this is not a trick for anyone who doesn't have a great deal of time to put into training his pet. The dog must be absolutely perfect in his basic training and have complete trust in his owner, wanting to please him as much as he can, or else it will be unsafe for him. Don't think you can just go out one afternoon and do this trick with your dog, thinking it might be fun. This trick is potentially dangerous, and if done incorrectly, it could kill your dog. Follow my directions carefully, or don't do it.

34 Obedience Trials, Movies, and Commercials

This book has covered most obedience feats required for kennel-club obedience trials. The American Kennel Club is the oldest known dog organization in the United States and the most organized. I like to use some of their training standards, since my clients derive great pleasure out of taking their dogs to AKC obedience trials and seeing them work in competition with other dogs. And I also enjoy seeing dogs that I have trained performing well.

For rules and format of these trials, please contact the AKC. Find out what is expected of you from the different obedience trials and adjust the training accordingly.

After you receive the information on regulations from the AKC, you will notice that everything that a dog is expected to do, from the lowest obedience class to the highest, is in some way covered in this book. Unfortunately, it is really very difficult to explain the exact format of these obedience trials. I could give you a schedule of all the exercises your dog is expected to perform at each level of competition. But the only way to know exacty what is expected of you and your dog is to go to obedience trials and watch for yourself.

When you are showing your dog, however, I advise that you put him through his paces for about fifteen minutes before the trial starts so that his repertoire is fresh in his mind. I also advise that he be completely housebroken, because your dog can get disqualified if he relieves himself in the ring. So walk him first.

Getting a dog to perform tricks before the camera is, again, simply a matter of linking basic commands taught in this book. However, the main problem with commercials and movies is that a dog usually has to perform a feat twenty or thirty times in a row, or rather, the trainer has to be able to make him. From what you know now of a dog's capacity for boredom, you can see that this is not easy.

The heat of the lights is another problem for animals that are supposed to appear cool and collected.

A dog often misbehaves on the set for the same exact reasons he does in a new locale. There are odd sounds, strange smells, new people, and often other dogs to contend with. On a commercial I was shooting, a problem developed when the dog moved his bowels on the set. A reading of the union rules was required to determine whose responsibility it was to clean it up. It turned out that it was the responsibility of the gaffer, or electrician, until it hit the ground—whereupon the responsibility fell on the prop man.

I use "rapid" training for film and commercial use. This training is not merely in the interests of speed, but to overcome the myriad distractions that conspire to reduce a dog's attention span. By using this technique, I don't give the animals time to make mistakes while they're getting the routine down pat. By the time they get around to testing my authority, they have done what the script calls for, for as many times as the director wants, and the commercial or film has been shot. In addition, most of the dogs I work with belong to my clients and as I've worked with these dogs before, I have established a working rapport with them. So I can't help but get good results.

Most commercials demand constant improvising, because the more you get the dog to perform, the more the director wants. For one commercial, all Inches was supposed to do was bark at a mailman. On the final cut, he would be wearing the mailman's hat, standing up on his hind legs, and delivering a letter.

Basically, I use the same techniques in training for commercials and films as taught in this book. However, when dogs are in the act, you must get the shot when you can, because a dog's attention span is limited. And, unlike humans, the concept of "stardom" is not an incentive.

Of course, there are stock shots that are accomplished through little tricks. These include such things as clapping your hands to make a dog's ears perk up, the sight of another dog to make a dog look excited, or a firm "no" off camera to make a dog's ears droop. When recording live, however, one cannot make any noise at all, and this is where our hand commands play an important role.

Most TV and movie tricks are within your dog's capacity. The only problem is that unless you understand the actual mechanics of film-making, you can't really do a thorough job.

To many producers and directors, the dogs are animated scenery, and only the human actors are religiously referred to as "the talent." Many production companies don't care about the dog, just the movie. An inconsiderate production assistant will often order up food and drink for the cast but nothing for the tired, overheated animals. Often directors want a fairly realistic dogfight—you know, the heroic dog protecting his master from the villain's German shepherd. And they assume that because an animal can be trained to "play" with a human actor in a way that looks pretty grisly on camera, two dogs can "play" with each other in an equally convincing manner. What they don't understand is that full-grown dogs don't play with strange dogs, not even with friendly ones until dominance has been established. Two dogs encouraged to sic each other can easily get carried away, and at least one of them will get hurt.

I have always made sure that all of my animal talent are treated humanely. There really is no entertainment value to be gotten from seeing animals misused, so I refuse to work when an animal has to be hurt in order to make him perform, or must work under dangerous conditions.

If you want your pet to be used in movies or commercials, here are a few pointers:

• Make sure that he is thoroughly obedience trained and trick trained.

• Be cautious of "acting classes" for dogs. Thorough obedience training never hurt any dog, but make sure that the school he goes to is a reputable one. There are far too many trainers around who take advantage of people's love for their dogs.

• Register him with *reliable* animal talent agencies, production companies, and ad agencies. Include in his resumé a picture and all relevant information like size, color, etc. Also list the tricks he can do.

• Remember that your main reward will be personal

satisfaction rather than money. Always keep in mind that dogs do not receive residuals from commercials and that agents should and do take a fee.

• If your dog is performing, and if you are not a professional trainer, it may be better for you to stay away from the shooting entirely. You may only get in the way.

For example, Inches had gotten used to looking for my wife, Jo, and following her cues only. Not only did he refuse to perform at my commands, but did a few leg lifts on the set as well. Jo left, and the problem was solved. Inches could now concentrate on his work and not her.

If your dog will perform for you, he should do just as well with an on-set trainer. Besides, you won't be missing much if you do stay away. A location is usually a fairly dull place, with many different people milling about but very little apparently being accomplished. Once the cameras begin to roll, the scene is usually repeated again and again, to the point of savage tedium to anyone not directly involved. So if you do attend, leave the day free, and bring a good book.

35 Attack Dogs . . .

Muggings and burglaries have reached epidemic proportions in most cities, and even in suburbia. Dogs have always been great at holding off intruders, of course, and many owners choose their pets for exactly this purpose. One New Yorker has two Dobermans—one for home and one to keep watch on his car. With a Doberman sitting right inside, who's going to bother it, or even think of stealing? Another career lady takes her pug along to the movies for protection. Young girls walking after midnight feel more carefree in the wake of a burly mastiff.

So popular is the watchdog-security theory that intrepid American marketers have invented mechanical watchdog devices for empty homes. The intruder steps on the welcome mat, touching off a tape of a dog barking. It's fine until the recording gets scratched or stops in midbark. But most security-minded people want the real thing, an honest-to-God attack-trained guard god, and it is here that they make a potentially tragic mistake.

Attack dogs were originally trained to fight each other for sport, or to run messages and fight against other attack dogs in wartime. But with airplanes and tanks doing our fighting for us these days, attack dogs have moved to a new battleground and a new enemy, the criminal.

Attack trainers often claim that their methods are "humane," but there is no humane way to make a dog attack human beings on command. The training used to be humane, inasmuch as the dog was simply left to his own natural protective devices. But as crime rates prove, it is increasingly hard to trust anyone, and so modern attack dogs have to be trained to see every human being as an immediate threat to be dispatched. Today's attack-dog-to-be is teased by a "professional agitator," tied to a pole and beaten, shouted at, put in a dark room where things he cannot see are hurled at him—and finally made to think that he will be physically hurt if he *doesn't* attack. Once the dog has the confidence to take on his antagonists, his master frequently can only "control" him by belting him with a length of chain. An attack dog's lot is hardly better than a prisoner of war's, and they are treated in cruelly similar ways. And this is just the damage you do to the dog. Anyone in his vicinity is a potential victim.

The danger of owning an attack-trained dog is no secret In some states, and it should be true in all, such dogs come under special regulatory laws, mostly because of their liability factor. You must notify the local fire, police, and animal-regulations departments so that they will be aware of your dog if they should have some emergency proceedings on your property. A courageous fireman or policeman has enough on his mind.

A strange voice rang me up and asked: "Can you train dogs to attack?" I asked him why he wanted one and told him that I don't like to train attack dogs unless it's absolutely necessary. The caller's answer was hard to believe: "Just in case somebody bothers me, I want the dog to rip his eyes out!" I hung up.

Often the individuals who want such an animal are frustrated fighters, living out their particular physical fantasies through their dogs, so they are a hundred times more dangerous than they are protective. Whom are they protecting from whom? The dog can get confused about this too.

Attack dogs are trained to kill and maim—these are their main commands. Sometimes training stops before the dog is completely trained. He just knows how to bark and bite uncontrollably. What is usually neglected is thorough basic obedience training.

Many are trained to attack anyone who lifts his hand as if to strike the animal or his master. Even if he doesn't tear into some little boy waving at a friend across the street, he will be constantly on the lookout for his cue, ready to "perform" on anyone who shows "aggression" that is only in his mind.

What makes people think they can handle this kind of

a dog? Owners learn by trial and error, and sometimes by accident. I train attack dogs only when I feel it's absolutely necessary, such as when I receive a request from law-enforcement agencies. However, I am beginning to wonder about the necessity for anyone's owning an attack-trained dog. It's like owning a loaded gun. It's necessary to control the attack dog continuously, and few people have enough control of themselves—let alone a trained killer.

The male dog is a dominant animal, and the master is teaching him to become more so by attacking his human companion. Therefore, the creature is even more likely than a normal dog to test his master. Even if you're not lax on discipline, at five and six years of age, attack dogs know how to handle *you*, and there's an excellent chance that once an attack dog reaches his peak, he will turn on his master.

One New York department store employs seven Dobermans to guard its premises and a trainer who takes care of them full time. During the day the dogs relax in a cage on the roof, and roam the store by night. One day while their trainer was feeding them in the penthouse enclosure, two dogs started a fight over a contested chunk of beef. When the trainer attempted to break them up, they forgot their mutual differences and turned on him. He was badly bitten, and only a fast rush and a slam of the enclosure door saved his life.

If an attack dog's target has little experience with such beasts, he'll have no chance of remaining in one piece. Even if you're a professional, and you know the right clues to when he's making a move, you're going to be in for it. When any dog's ready to test you, he'll make some aggressive gesture that may appear fairly innocuous. We've covered the significance of a leg lift, and a growl is obvious. But ironically, the indications that an attack dog *really* means business are not so obvious.

A straight, unwavering gaze, lowered ears, rising hackles are all early-warning signs, but not *always* displayed by a dog about to lunge. Hackles are usually raised when a dog is frightened or angry. If he's about to attack you in cold blood, he often won't bother to raise his hackles. The definitive thing to watch for is the dog's body movements. A dog will begin moving stiffly, almost on tiptoe, his whole body contracting and tensing into one huge fist.

He's quietly checking out each muscle, getting ready to move instantly, whenever he sees his best chance.

If a hostile dog is faced with several possible human targets, he will usually go with the strongest odor. We sweat both when we're angry and when we're frightened. A dog does not discriminate between your anger and your fear. All he knows is that the most "emotional" figure is probably the most motivated, and hence the greater risk to him, so he'll go for that one first.

If you must have an attack dog, follow the pattern adopted by most attack trainers. Have only *one* dog. (More than one constitutes a pack.) And be with that one constantly. The person who wants this type of dog should be present for months and months of intensive training with him. In fact, he should be with the dog continually, because a well-trained animal should attack and withdraw only at his master's command. One attack trainer has kept his "floor sample" attack dog with him day and night for nine years, and gives it constant commands for other, less lethal tricks, to emphasize how supposedly docile the dog is.

When attack training is necessary for law enforcement or the military, I suggest using only a female dog. A male will look to take over the pack. He has a way of testing you and knowing enough about you to take you on. More of a companion, the female dog thinks more of protecting her master than of attacking his enemies (or him). She doesn't have any domineering plans. She is more gentle, very much wants to please and follow your instructions.

If the whole idea of an attack-trained dog still appeals to you, please be aware of all the dangers and responsibilities. And remember, too, that a clever burglar can easily defend himself against most attack dogs. Some trainers teach dogs to attack by using a padded sleeve to agitate them. Naturally, the dog learns to go for the sleeve *only*, leaving himself wide open for a blow on the head.

One owner had trained his dog to attack whenever a stranger approached with his hand raised in a threatening gesture. "Pretend you're going to attack him," he invited. I simply pointed my index finger at the dog and cocked my thumb: "Bang!" The dog never budged, and faced with a revolver, he wouldn't have had a chance to. On the other hand, a child waving his hand playfully *would* elicit this dog's attack response.

Attack dogs have other built-in weak spots too. All an enterprising burglar need do is introduce a tiny (and easily portable) female in heat to the dog-patrolled premises, and his worries are over. A single attack dog will rather make love than war, and in the presence of a female, two or more male attack dogs will literally annihilate each other! This is another reason why I advise using females for attack training, if at all—not only are they more ready to accept commands and easier to control than males, but they are also immune to seduction.

There's still another drawback, in that an attack dog remains what he has been taught to become—a savage, unpredictable beast—virtually forever. He'll never retire into being a family pet, never be a companion you can play and relax with. An attack-trained dog cannot roam free in the house or behave like a normal dog. If he's ever to be returned to society, his detraining, by necessity, has to be more brutal than the original attack training.

The dog's original confidence has to be sapped, completely. Here's where I have to employ an electric collar —to save my life. There's a separate transmitter that can be activated simply by pressing a button. For shock-collar training, a dog should be fitted first with a dummy collar resembling the real thing so he won't associate the new collar with punishment. The dog is fitted with the real collar and then commanded to attack. As soon as he lunges, press the button on the transmitter and hold the charge until the dog stops his attack. This is unpleasant, but don't blame me. Blame whoever attack-trained the dog in the first place. The procedure is repeated until the dog no longer attacks on command; literally, until he becomes afraid of people. But unlike the "conditioning" administered to the violence-prone Alex in *A Clockwork Orange*, this detraining is not based on conditioned response. That is, the dog learns to be *consciously* shy, while his earlier attack-training is simply repressed, buried beneath a new set of "lessons."

But still there is no guarantee that he won't relapse into his old habits when he gets spontaneously carried away. Or he may simply decide to test his master, as all dogs do, at a time when the electric collar is safely packed away. Unfortunately, the only way to be sure of a former attack dog is to have him put to sleep.

All of which helps to explain why I ask people to think twice before embarking on attack-training a dog. Think of what you're doing to the animal. Even if he is later de-trained, he'll always be afraid of you, incapable of ever being a lovable, trustworthy pet. And quite literally, your loss may be greater than his.

Attack dogs must be for professionals only. Don't let yourself be taken in by the occasional unscrupulous trainer who says you need an attack dog for protection, and tries to sell you one for many hundreds of dollars.

36 . . . Versus
Defense Pets

Does the preceding diatribe against attack dogs mean that you shouldn't consider getting a dog to help ward off evildoers? Not at all. Just the sight of anyone with a large dog makes your run-of-the-mill mugger think twice.

One lady was letting her wholly docile sheepdog relieve himself in the space between two cars on a darkened street. As she stood on the sidewalk, letting the six-foot leash go slack, two thugs sauntered up and snarled, "Give us your money."

"I'll give you *this*," she said, jerking the leash in one swift pull. When her previously unseen dog bounded into view, her attackers fled. The point is that many criminals are afraid of *any* dog. As long as attack dogs do exist, no miscreant can be sure that your dog *isn't* one. And, therefore, he doesn't really have to be.

There are certain exceptions to this rule, of course. One of my clients was mugged while walking his dog on Fourteenth Street. The dog barked and growled to no avail, while the mugger took the owner's wallet and fled. I had to explain to him that not everybody is scared of four-pound dogs. Another owner's pet was so docile that he emitted his first growl only *after* his owner had been held up.

However, muggers have often admitted they would never go after anyone with a dog, however small. And the presence of a dog, of any size, inside your home is still more of a discouragement to a prospective felon, who may just choose the peace and quiet of the place next door. A small Pekingese is not as helpful as a giant mastiff,

215

but he can still make a painful dent in an intruder's leg. Quite obviously, the major factor in any dog's "protective" ability is bluff, and a good "front" can be instilled in any dog without actually turning it into a killer. And just a dog of the right breed can automatically spell "danger":

> *Now the Doberman had the driver of the . . . truck backed up against his cab, screeching hysterically. . . . It was clear that he felt he was about to be chewed up and killed, for no reason at all, by some vicious animal that had come out of the darkness. . . .*
>   —Hunter S. Thompson

The Doberman pinscher's reputation as an attack and terror dog was one of the Germans' most successful propaganda campaigns, because even today many people are frightened just by the sight of this dog. The owners of even the most docile Dobermans will tell you that people always ask them if their dogs are vicious or have ever turned on them.

The Doberman was first bred to be a very vicious dog. A nervous greyhound bitch was bred for her speed and aggressiveness to a male Rottweiler for his strength. The resultant dog was a Doberman pinscher. His tail and ears were clipped for two reasons: first, to make him appear Satanic, and secondly, to give a human no chance to grab hold of him and stop his attack. The truth of the matter is that if you left the ears alone, the Doberman pinscher would be a lovable-looking dog.

This is not to say that a Doberman can't do any damage, but so can other breeds. It's just that the Doberman has the reputation of being the "hell's angel" of the dog world. For sheer menacing appearance, a German shepherd takes second place.

I train many dogs to bark on a signal from their owners. These dogs are called guard dogs.* It often makes people feel safer when out walking to know that their dog will bark on command. The sound of barking dogs can be very reassuring wherever crime rates are a problem. I like my dogs to bark when they are left alone in my apart-

---

* *My* guard dogs are trained to growl, bark, and generally appear aggressive. They are *not* vicious and will *not* attack. However, in some training schools "guard" and "attack" mean the same thing. So check to be sure.

ment. Including Plum, there are four of them in there (plus Martha, the parrot, who has also learned to bark, if not quite as ferociously). My immediate neighbors are only too happy to have my gang sound off at the approach of the elevator. I like them to bark so the place doesn't get robbed. But even a burglar alarm needs a turnoff switch, and when I raise my voice above the din to tell them to *shut up!* they do. (If I'm not there, they keep on with the noise, but then, so does a burglar alarm.)

Induce barking by making a game out of it. You might open an umbrella and make movements toward your dog. His first bark will be in fright. After he barks, back up. This will give him the confidence to test you the next time, to see if you'll back up when he barks. You're giving him confidence, because after all, you keep backing up. You might try covering your face with your arm, like a bandit. Play with him. But when he barks of his own accord, cover his mouth with your hand and say "no." Teach him to bark only when you want him to.

To train your dog to bark at others, have a friend cover his face with a coat or umbrella and make aggressive motions and sounds at the dog. At the same time nudge your dog forward, saying "watch him"—or whatever command word you prefer. When the dog starts to bark, have your friend quickly back away. This will give the dog confidence. Praise your dog and say "good boy." Eventually the dog will connect the command "watch him" with barking. Work this exercise no more than ten minutes per day. Be patient, it takes time.

A barking dog is not a good deterrent for an "inside job" burglary. If a burglar wanted to rob this apartment, his best move would be to visit me four or five times, stop in, say hello, and leave. The dogs would still bark when he entered later, but not as emphatically as they would if he were a total stranger. Of course, they would also be familiar to *him*, and he wouldn't be frightened by noise alone.

One of my favorite tricks is to instruct nine-pound Inches to "guard this with your life." A diamond brooch, or a dog-eared TV *Guide*, it doesn't matter. I simply drop the object at Inches' feet. If anyone, on four legs or two, approaches, Inches begins furious barking and snarling, and he's built low enough to the ground to defend his claim. If I tell Plum to "go get that from Inches," Plum approaches, gets barked at, and retreats.

This "defense" training was simple. I simply made a few moves toward Inches' personal toys, leather bones, and goods, on various occasions. Inches was praised for showing aggression *when told to,* but I made it clear that barking was the limit. In short, I transformed the dog's natural defensive reaction into a trick that was under my control. Inches knew that he wasn't really supposed to hold the line at any cost. It was a game. But a visitor or casual stranger does not see the "trick." Inches' barking and my sinister command create the proper atmosphere.

37 Sniffing Out Bombs and Drugs

This type of training is used mostly by the armed services and law-enforcement agencies across the country. A dog with his keen sense of smell and never-ending nosing around can be more efficient than some of the most sophisticated devices man can conjure up.

Marijuana and hashish contain a particularly aromatic resin that a dog can detect quite easily. Unless you repeatedly wash your hands and wrap your stash in layers of plastic bags, it's almost impossible to avoid transferring some of this resin to the outside of your container, where a dog can detect it. But so can you, once it's burning, and so pot-sniffing is really not a terribly practical sideline for your dog, unless you plan to use him to amuse and disconcert your counter-culture friends.

Sniffing out marijuana and hashish puts your dog in no possible danger. On the other hand, with the harder drugs such as heroin, there is a distinct possibility of the dog's becoming addicted, because you have to train him with samples of actual drugs you want him to seek out. It is pretty silly to try to get a dog to sniff out cocaine because this drug will freeze his sense of smell and he won't even be able to smell himself.

During World War II, the Germans used to send attack-trained Dobermans out after refugees trying to escape across the mountains into neutral territory. The underground would mix dried blood powder with cocaine and leave small heaps of this mixture in the escapees' wake. When the dogs, alerted by the smell of blood, paused to sniff the stuff more closely, they got enough of a dose of "nose candy" to throw them safely off the trail. So to make a long story short, a dog who can sniff out bombs or any other explosive devices probably benefits society the most. Paradoxically, this is not a particularly dangerous pastime. A bomb sniffer is trained to point at, rather than dig for, the explosive.

First of all, you need a perfectly obedience-trained dog no younger than eighteen months. Make sure that he is a friendly dog, and definitely not one that is attack- or guard-trained. If you use an attack dog, you will be too busy worrying that he might bite somebody. Moreover, an attack dog often becomes aggressive when his handler, or the suspect he's sniffing, smells the least bit nervous or uneasy.

People have heard so many stories about tireless blood-hounds scent-tracking for hundreds of miles that they don't realize these dogs must be *trained* for such feats. Sporting dogs, retrievers, and hounds do rely on scent, but they still have to become excited before they'll take off after whatever they're tracking. In other words, a dog must have a motive beyond the mere thrill of the chase, at least initially.

In order to have a perfect bomb-sniffer, you must work your dog with more patience than in any other trick. I say "trick" because to the dog, finding a bomb is just another way for him to get his reward, and in this type of training, as you will see, he gets his reward from the person he searches as well as from the handler. I like to use hounds or retrievers in this type of work because their sense of smell is the keenest of all breeds.

If you want a dog to trace or seek out a bomb that contains gun-powder, it's the smell of the sulfur that you should concentrate on first, because not only is sulfur the strongest-scented of all the ingredients in gunpowder, but by using only this one ingredient by itself in training, you won't be risking an explosion.

Take a convenient but leakproof object, such as a card-board box, a loosely capped glass jar, or a canvas bag, and fill it with sulfur. You want to be sure that some of the odor can escape, but that the sulfur won't actually spill out into your dog's mouth when he goes to fetch the object to you.

Get your dog used to retrieving this object by both sight and smell, then start to secrete it in places where he has to depend on his sense of smell to find it—tall grass is good for a start. At the beginning, remember to show your dog the general area where you threw the object, so he can have some idea of where to start sniffing. Every time he finds the object for you, you must reward him. A good procedure is to make him find the object before giving him his food each day. When he is perfect at this, then put the object into a bag or box. Let your dogs see you doing this, tell him to "fetch" the object, and give him the command to "seek" or "find." When he obeys, even though he saw you hide it, give him plenty of praise.

Now take three small suitcases, all of the same size and shape. Place them a few feet apart. Sit your dog facing the suitcases, but a few feet away, and let him watch you place the object in one of the three. It's very important that you let him see which bag you're putting the object in. Now close all three, walk away, and tell him to "find" or "seek." Praise him when he picks the right one.

When he gets this down pat, then start to mix the bags up, while keeping the object in *one* bag. You don't want all three bags smelling of sulfur. Don't be too surprised when he picks the right one each time, but praise him anyway. Once he has done this perfectly, then try placing the object on a person. When and if the dog finds it, you must reward him and let the person who has the object reward him. This way he will eagerly search any person you send him to, because as far as he is concerned, he is going to get a double reward.

It's now time for you to try him with the real thing. Rather than mix the powder yourself, use shotgun shells, with the pellets out and a Band-Aid over the primer just for good measure. As usual, if your dog is weak at any point of the training, go back to the last step he performed correctly and work forward from there.

Once you have him perfectly trained, you must let him find the object each time, even if you are using him to search out a real bomb. In other words, work him for a short time, then have somebody put an object containing gunpowder in his pocket or in a bag. Let your dog find it, then reward him. If you don't, he will get tired of being "fooled" and won't work for you.

Obviously, this same training procedure will work equally well for teaching a dog to sniff out drugs. Nor is there any reason that your dog cannot learn to sniff out *both* bombs and dope, *as long as he is taught to seek one*

perfectly before being sicced on a second material. Because a dog's nose is particularly sensitive to acids, it will be easier for him to detect a bomb manufactured from nitroglycerin, which contains nitric acid. But because the two odors are different, you should alternate the nitric acid with sulfur, which your dog already recognizes, switching the two each new lesson, until your dog responds equally to either scent.

Part Five

FROM
BIRTH
TO
DEATH

38 Selecting Your Puppy

"Is there a right breed for me?"

No, there isn't. But there is a right *dog,* and after reading my book I feel that you should be able to handle just about any dog if you follow my examples properly.

As I don't know you personally or anything about your family setup, I don't feel I'm in any position to give a cut-and-dried answer as to what breed is right for you. Dogs differ in both temperament and personality just as humans do, so I can't tell you to get a specific breed because it will definitely have certain characteristics. What the breed was *originally* bred for won't tell you what it is used for today.

There are many basic different breeds of dogs which can be divided into six groups, according to the purposes for which they were originally bred:

1. *Sporting dogs.* Most of these were originally bred as bird dogs. However, some in this category were also used for larger game. This group consists of the following:

Wirehaired pointing griffin	*Gordon setter*
English pointer	*Irish setter*
German shorthaired pointer	*American water spaniel*
German wirehaired pointer	*Brittany spaniel*
Chesapeake Bay retriever	*Clumber spaniel*
Curly-coated retriever	*Cocker spaniel*
Flat-coated retriever	*English cocker spaniel*
Golden retriever	*English springer spaniel*
Yellow Labrador retriever	*Welsh springer spaniel*
Black Labrador retriever	*Vizsla*
English setter	*Weimaraner*

2. *Hounds.* These are split into two categories, consisting of sight hounds and scent hounds. Both were originally hunting dogs used for trailing and killing fur-bearing game. Sight hounds hunted primarily by using their sight and speed, as opposed to the scent hounds who used their sense of smell.

SIGHT GROUP	SCENT GROUP
Afghan hound	*Basset hound*
Basenji	*Beagle*
Borzoi	*Bloodhound*
Scottish deerhound	*Black and tan coonhound*
Greyhound	*Dachshund*
Irish wolfhound	*American foxhound*
Saluki	*English foxhound*
Whippet	*Harrier*
	Norwegian elkhound
	Otterhound
	Rhodesian ridgeback

3. *Working Dogs.* They were bred to perform working tasks for their human masters such as protecting, shepherding, sled pulling, and even mountain rescue.

Alaskan malamute	*Kuvasz*
Belgian sheepdog	*Mastiff*
Tervuren	*Newfoundland*
Burmese mountain dog	*Old English sheepdog*
Bouvier des Flandres	*Puli*
Boxer	*Rottweiler*
Briard	*Samoyed*
Bull mastiff	*Schnauzer*
Collie (rough and smooth)	*(giant and standard)*
Doberman pinscher	*Shetland sheepdog*
German shepherd	*Siberian husky*
Great Dane	*St. Bernard*
Great Pyrenees	*Welsh corgi*
Komondor	*(short and long hair)*

4. *Terriers.* These breeds were originally bred as ratters, fighting dogs, and/or to ferret out underground animals.

Airedale terrier	*Lakeland terrier*
Australian terrier	*Manchester terrier*
Bedlington terrier	*Miniature schnauzer*
Border terrier	*Scottish terrier*
Bull terrier	*Sealyham terrier*
Cairn terrier	*Skye terrier*
Dandie Dinmont terrier	*Staffordshire terrier*
Fox terrier	*Welsh terrier*
Irish terrier	*West Highland terrier*
Kerry blue terrier	

5. *Toys.* These are, as is apparent from their name, strictly pets. They are usually small in size and many have been bred down from larger breeds.

Affenpinscher	*Miniature pinscher*
Chihuahua	*Pomeranian*
English toy spaniel	*Silky terrier*
Brussels griffin	*Toy poodle*
Italian greyhound	*Pug*
Japanese spaniel	*Toy Manchester terrier*
Maltese (spaniel)	*Shih Tzu*
Papillon	*Yorkshire terrier*
Pekingese	

6. *Nonsporting Dogs.* This group includes an assortment of breeds that do not specifically fit into any of the other groups because they were used for various purposes at various times.

Boston terrier	*Keeshond*
Bulldog	*Lhasa apso*
Chow	*Poodle*
Dalmatian	*Schipperke*
French bulldog	

From within these groups, pick out the breed you think is right for you. Then go to dog shows and research it thoroughly. If you are choosing a dog for performance, go to the obedience trials. Your local newspapers have notices as to where and when these shows are held. But don't forget that the dogs here are very well disciplined, most of them are professionally trained and handled, and you may well see any breed at all walking off with the first prize.

After doing this, send away to your local kennel clubs for information regarding breeders. Go out and visit them and learn all you can. When you are completely convinced that you have selected the right breed for you and your family, *then* it's time for you to buy a puppy, take him home, love him, and train him.

A popular misconception is that inbreeding results in inferior dogs. Actually, inbreeding is quite healthy if the principle of natural selection, or reproduction of the fittest, is maintained. In a pack, the animals inbreed. Mixed breeds are often strong, healthy dogs because they are the product of relatively natural selection. Their fathers couldn't have been too inferior, or else they would have never been sired in the first place. If you were to take a pack of dogs and let them roam together, it would be the strongest dogs who would control the pack and therefore reproduce themselves. A strain of dogs often begins to deteriorate when the dogs are bred for a particular quality and other attributes are disregarded.

In a number of breeds, the dog's "natural" attributes are working against him. Great Danes, for instance, were originally bred in England as guard dogs for the palaces of the nobility. Because the breeders were after sheer size and weight, today's Great Dane is equipped with a body too heavy for his long, spindly legs, and a heart simply too small for his entire carriage. This is why Great Danes seldom live for more than nine years. Their hearts give out. Even before this time, the sheer weight of the Dane's massive chest and head will induce arthritis in his relatively underdeveloped legs. The movements of a young Dane restrict themselves to an awkward rolling gait, as if the dog were walking on thin ice. It's not pain, simply the deterioration of the muscles and joints.

Similarly, the drooping eyelids of a basset or bloodhound have been exaggerated through selective breeding. Because of his sheer length, a dachshund is prone to back problems. You should never pick him up by the front legs, or exert undue pressure on the center of his spine. Bedlington terriers have been bred to develop increasingly small, narrow skulls—as fashion dictates that they look more in proportion that way. They are literally breeding their brains out.

To make the whole picture even worse, at the moment in this country there exist puppy "factories" known as breeding farms. Strictly production-line operations, they produce as many purebred puppies as they possibly can without any consideration of how the pups will turn out.

Many years ago it was the cocker spaniel that won most people's hearts. Then it was the poodle, which is still very popular for pet shows and breeding. Lap dogs are getting lots of attention now, especially the Yorkshire and silky terriers. There's a run on huskies right now, and the puppy mills follow these fashions quite closely, mating even the inferior animals to keep up with the public demand. Once a breed becomes very popular, the puppy farms really start rolling them out, and this has caused the ruin of many of the previously better breeds.

Hip dysplasia is only one of the conditions which have become commonplace since uncontrolled breeding took over. Proper breeding will eliminate this genetically transmitted weakness from future litters of shepherds, Labradors, collies, St. Bernards, Newfoundlands, Burmese mountain dogs and, in fact, most of the larger breeds. The animal's hips (pelvic area) become so dislocated that it is in constant pain, though the only observable symptoms may be difficulty in moving about and a penchant for lying down. I have seen dogs so badly afflicted that they seldom walked at all.

There are, of course, many reputable breeders who are very interested in the quality of the puppies they produce. Quantity is not their business, but quality. You usually find such breeders frequenting the dog shows sponsored by the large dog organizations. In fact, many breeds have an organization devoted strictly to the perfection of their particular breed.

There are many reputable pet shops also, and these are the people to buy your puppy from. Take the advice of your vet or someone you know who got a good dog. Check around and pick carefully. Save yourself later regrets. People often settle for a cute dog in the window and within a few weeks become very attached. Therefore, it is important that you get a healthy puppy at the start.

The only things you can really check on in buying a pup are his physical health, looks, and heredity. The rest is up to you, including his temperament. Be sure that he's alert, lively, friendly, and full of pep. A good pet shop will be glad to tell you where the puppy was bred, who the dam and the sire were and, if they were susceptible breeds, whether they were X-rayed for hip dysplasia. Unfortunately, hip dysplasia cannot be detected until a puppy reaches about six months of age, and therefore the X-rays of the dam and the sire are of great importance. In addition, try to find out the parents' temperament.

Any reputable breeder or pet shop will give you this information. If they will not or cannot furnish this, you should get a guarantee as to the quality of your puppy. This will prevent the heartache of having to live with or destroy a physically disabled dog.

The seller should grant *both* (a) a short-term guarantee (until the dog is checked by a vet) that the puppy is healthy and free of any diseases, and (b) a lifetime guarantee against congenital defects (deafness, hip dysplasia, etc.).

We're not talking about the beauty of a dog, but about actual physical impairments that could be prevented through proper breeding. If more people were to check the quality of the pup before buying, all breeders would soon be forced to start breeding quality dogs. Once you buy a dog, a veterinarian's checkup should be scheduled the next day.

Your vet will tell you when to bring your dog in for his rabies, distemper, leptospirosis, and hepatitis inoculations. (Rabies is now a very rare disease in dogs. But keep it that way by making sure he gets his rabies shot regularly.)

People say certain breeds of dogs look much better if their ears are cropped. But I don't think cropping of ears is a health advantage to any dog. As for looks, I can see some people getting their own noses fixed to make themselves more attractive to the opposite sex, but the head is the last place a dog looks when he is expecting to make love.

Some people say that a dog may get his ears or tail

ripped off in a fight, but it makes better sense to keep the dog from fighting. The tail of a happy Labrador can easily make a clean sweep of a low coffee table, of course, but it's easy to keep breakables out of wagging range. Tails or ears should be removed only if the dog has something wrong with them.

It's not hard to hear of someone who is offering a grown purebred for free. But there are certain things to look for and ask about when adopting a grown dog. Almost *nobody* gives away a well-trained dog, so you can bet that the "good deal" you're getting has one of three things definitely wrong with him:

1. He's a biter. Not only that, he has recently bitten someone. The present owner is frightened or about to be sued and has to get rid of him, and if he tells you he bites, you won't take him.

2. He's a chronic chewer and has eaten up the house, which, again, the present owner won't tell you.

3. The dog has not been housebroken—which again . . .

A chronic chewer can be cured, and a dog can be housebroken. But if the dog is a biter, I suggest that you either hire, or become, an experienced trainer, because the biting dog can pose a very dangerous problem to you and your family. You're not going to stop this habit with just plain love and simple discipline.

I'm not saying that you will never be offered a perfectly well-behaved dog for adoption. The original owner could very well be moving to a country such as England, New Zealand, or Australia, where there are very strong, six-to nine-month quarantine laws. In such a case, I can see trying to get the dog a good home in the States. But the above are the commonest reasons for an owner's getting rid of a grown animal.

The usual time for giving away unwanted dogs is just before or just after the summer, when the family is about to leave for vacation or about to be forced to move the dog indoors.

The dogs in a pound are almost always healthy, because the animals have been given a physical examination before being released to new owners. They will be young dogs, under three years old, and come from various sources: off the streets or from owners who have been forced (often by city housing regulations) to give up their animals. You may find many pedigreed dogs in a pound as well as mixed breeds, but the papers to prove it, of course, will almost always be lacking.

39 To Breed
or Not to Breed

What about breeding puppies all your own? I feel most
people jump into breeding without having any knowledge
of the problems involved. Eight puppies in a three-room
apartment can be a big problem—just think about it.

Some want their dogs to be happy parents. Others feel
that breeding will make their dogs more mature and stop
males from mounting their guests' arms and legs. But in
reality, this is a sign of aggression, and the only way to
stop it is with obedience training. In a pack situation,
mounting by the male is not always the result of a sexual
urge. (Research with the stickleback fish has proved that
the male mating instinct and aggression are hopelessly
intermeshed, and this association of sexual behavior with
self-assertion seems universal throughout the animal king-
dom.) Males will mount other males simply to assert dominance and rank, and since the dominant males of a pack
forbid the weaker males to touch the packs' females,
submissive males will often mount one another out of
sheer frustration. Homosexuality as understood by humans simply does not exist among canines.

Still others breed their dogs in the hopes of making
money. They usually end up with a litter they can't sell,
and they give the pups to friends, which is fine, or put
them in a pet shop on consignment, which isn't. It doesn't
make sense that owners insist on breeding more puppies
while abandoned dogs are being picked up daily by the
ASPCA.

Strays have had better times. During World War II,
retreating British soldiers picked up about eight hundred
homeless strays. The stray dogs were evacuated with their

rescuers at Dunkirk. But today, in Manhattan, there are regular spots where people dump unwanted dogs. All of Central Park is a deposit area, and the corner of West End Avenue and 96th Street is convenient because it adjoins the entrance to the West Side Highway.

These owners look simply for a spot that's relatively deserted and anonymous, free of witnesses who might make them feel guilty. People who discard their dogs often hope they'll "find new homes," but just how home-like is the corner of 96th and West End? People feel a dog off the street isn't worth anything. Of course, there are kindly folks who take in stray dogs, but their number is dwindling due to a labyrinthine list of financial and legal restrictions. As for those who are let go in the wild, chances are they won't survive. If they do, they could be-come part of a pack of wild dogs. These strays, and their offspring, are increasing far more quickly than owners can take them in.

The average age of a dog is about twelve years, and so this is the length of time it will take to solve the problem. Some have advocated putting birth control elements in dog food, but at the moment this method hasn't been proved safe, and the only means of population control is wholesale slaughter. Many people plant poison, espe-cially in parks, to kill stray dogs. One New Yorker elec-trocutes them in a homemade apparatus and feels that she's doing the right thing. And New York's Hatch-Metcalfe Law states that ASPCA dogs who are not adopted are either put to sleep or donated to laboratories.

I try to discourage mixed-breed litters, since most peo-ple buy pedigrees, and mixed breeds just aren't as wel-come in the world. With a purebred, you know what you're getting; with a mixed, you don't. Also, a purebred is worth money, and in this dollar-oriented society, this is what most people base their values on.

I have seen several prospective dog owners turn up their noses at a Pekingese. But after they were told the price of the dog, and discovered its close resemblance to the Fu dogs of Chinese porcelain, they saw it as a most handsome animal. When you go to the ASPCA to pick out a dog, you'll find that even there the dogs are divided into two sections—the mixed and the pedigrees. It would seem that prejudice also exists among the human-itarians.

Some owners justify mixed breeds as side products of their search for the "perfect" dog. However, anyone who tries to breed the "perfect" dog is headed for trouble. Tastes differ, and there will never be universal consensus on what an ideal dog should look like, act like, or be able to do.

Some mixed breeds can perform even better than some purebreds because of the mixture of the different qualities in the mixed breed, and as a matter of fact, all purebreds that were bred for particular jobs are a combination of other breeds. However, I don't recommend any kind of experimentation because it doesn't always work. There are plenty of purebreds with any number of abilities that you can now choose from.

Why *bother* to breed the perfect dog? Variety is the whole point and beauty of different breeds. Once you try to dictate people's taste, you're just wasting your time. On the other hand, the perfect dog of *any existing breed* is a worthwhile and plausible goal. I look for strength, physical fitness, and a good disposition in dogs, with looks running a poor fourth. The ideal Great Dane would be a smaller dog with a body more in proportion to its heart.

What crossbreeding has marred, it can also correct, and for this reason I am against the breeding of *purebreds* who are anything less than physically perfect. *If you don't want a litter on your hands, have your bitch spayed.* Many argue that it's more humane to let a dog sow its wild oats —but it would seem *more* humane to guarantee that all puppies would have proper homes, not left to forage in the streets and meet a violent, unnatural end. Spaying is *not* a major operation. Many dogs are spayed in the morning and back home again in the afternoon. Spaying is best performed when a female is about a year old, but check with your vet. Not only does it stop reproduction, it is also the best thing for a female as it prevents certain diseases of the uterus of the older female.

If your pet is a male, castration will not make him into a canine version of a docile eunuch, since all the energy he would otherwise expend in sex may well go into his instincts for territorial defense. But he won't chase heated females.

A little boy over on Park Avenue keeps telling his mother at odd times that his dog's lipstick is showing. This does not mean that the dog is sexually excited necessarily, merely that, as an extremely physical animal, he is showing his excitement or confusion through physical means. When a dog is being obedience trained, especially in the areas of "sit/stay" and "lie down," he cannot expend his energies by running around, so it comes out in the form of an erection.

For the owner of the unspayed female, one great source of aggravation is that period referred to as "in heat." The female comes into heat twice a year, and males in the vicinity are attracted by her characteristic odor. One ten-pound pug in heat was waiting with her mistress in front of a liquor-store counter. The German shepherd the store owner kept as a guard dog literally leaped the counter to reach the pug.

Many dismayed owners find that male dogs will chew and claw their way through wooden partitions to get at a heated female. Should more than one male dog arrive on the scene at once, they can go completely wild, wild enough, in fact, to kill one another. So the obvious answer is that a bitch in heat should be kept away from male dogs as much as possible.

You don't have to worry about secretions because dogs clean themselves. It doesn't hurt to keep alert for any abnormal discharge, but there's no reason to douche your dog unless your vet prescribes it for a specific medical problem.

If your purebred dog is physically perfect, you can obtain the name of a suitable mate through your local kennel club registry.* Usually the owners of a prize male stud will ask for a considerable fee, or depending on their own interest in breeding, on a specific number of pups. But if the heated female is brought to the male's house he will always urinate to reestablish his own territory. So, always have the stud dog do the visiting, never the female, and when the male has done his job, remove him immediately.

Make sure your pregnant dog isn't allowed on your bed or couch as she may choose those soft spots to give birth, later. About a week before the puppies are due, wash her teats to be sure they're clean as possible, so that the new-

---

* Then again, computerized dating services are springing up all over the country. One in Santa Monica bills itself as "Dog's Best Friend" and claims that it will "discover a compatible mate for your canine lover; arrange a romantic holiday."

born puppies will have a minimum of germs to contend with when they begin nursing. Whenever she begins looking about for paper or rags to make a nest, get her wherever you want her to be fast, because she and her puppies will be there for the next six weeks. Usually birth is a perfectly normal procedure, without undue problems, but keep an eye on her when she begins to give birth. If she seems to be having problems, call your vet immediately.

40 Epilogue

There are a few considerations to keep in mind when your dog begins aging. He won't be as physically agile or as much sheer fun as he was when younger. It's your responsibility to make him comfortable, to adapt to his needs. Don't overexercise him. Let him relax more. Take him for more frequent walks outside so his bladder doesn't have to duplicate the feats it did when he was younger.

When—or why—should a dog be put to sleep? Your veterinarian is the best judge, but the main reasons for putting dogs away are when they are in constant pain or dying. Most dogs die from aging of their vital organs such as heart, kidney, and liver. But proper care and understanding can prolong a happy life by many years. Even a severe physical disability does not necessarily mean your dog cannot live on with you. A blind dog, a deaf dog, even one missing a leg can be cared for adequately and is perfectly capable of enjoying whatever life and senses are left to him.

Animals *do* die, but that's something that most books don't point out. There are pet cemeteries, caskets, headstones—even funerals—available. But all of these things can't solace a bereaved owner as effectively as a new pet.

Gertrude Stein adored Basket, her white poodle. When he died, friends advised her to get another dog just like him. Picasso frowned on this idea, however, saying that a new white poodle would only remind her of the deceased Basket—"If I died, would you go out and find another Pablo?"—and suggested she buy an Afghan. Miss Stein simply replied, "The King is dead; long live the King!"

went to a dog show at the Porte de Versailles, and acquired a second white poodle whom she named Basket II.

If your last dog was a happy experience, it does seem a waste not to use the wisdom and experience you gathered from his training. You should be an even better master this time around, and it's hard to beat the joy and satisfaction of doing everything *right* from the very beginning.

INDEX

Adaptation
  absence of sweat glands as
      evolutionary, 33
  to human environment, 121-
      25
  loose-fitting skin as defen-
      sive, 32
Adolescent dogs, 30
Affenpinschers, 229
Afghans, 228
  eyesight of, 37
  as status dogs, 22
Aggressive behavior
  excrements and, 51
  odor camouflaging as, 39
  sexual instinct and, 235
  staring as, 52-53
  See also Territoriality
Aggressive dogs, 22, 119
Aging dogs, caring for, 240
Airedale terriers, 229
AKC (American Kennel
      Club), 205
Alaskan malamutes, 228
American foxhounds, 228
American Kennel Club
      (AKC), 205
American Society for the Pro-
      tection and Care of

Animals (ASPCA),
    235-36
American water spaniels, 199,
    227
Anatomy of dogs, 29-33
Anus-sniffing, 39
ASPCA (American Society for
    the Protection and Care
    of Animals), 235-36
Attack dogs, 209-14
  detraining, 213
  femal, 212-13
  sniffing bombs of drugs,
    219
  training of, 209-10
Australian terriers, 229
Authority figure, owner as, 18
Authority needed in training,
    137, 142

Babies, dogs and, 58-59
Bacterial endocarditis, 83
Barking, 108-11
  biting and, 114
  training for, 216
Basset hounds, 228, 230
Bathing, 34-36
Bazenjis, 228
Beagles, 228

Bedlington terriers, 229, 231
Belgian sheepdogs, 228
Bicycle riding with a leashed
    dog, 123
Bite pressure
    ability to control, 84
    strength of, 115
Biting, 114-17
    chronic, 117, 233
    frightened persons, 57
    growling and, 107
    by injured dogs, 116
    lack of training and, 26, 27
    nipping as, 114
    as sign of dominance, 52
Black Labrador retrievers, 227
Black and tan coonhounds,
    228
Bloodhounds, 228, 230
Body communication
    as greatest form of dog
        training, 173
    in reprimands, 71-75
Body odor of dogs, 33
Body temperature of puppies,
    29
Bombs, sniffing out, 219-23
Border terriers, 229
Borzois, 228
Boston terriers, 229
Bouviers des Flandres, 228
Boxers, 228
Breeding, 230-39
    effects of uncontrolled, 230-
        31
    inbreeding, 230
    mixed, 236-37
Briards, 228
Brittany spaniels, 227
Brushing, 35
Brussels griffins, 229
Bull mastiffs, 228
Bull terriers, 83, 229

Bulldogs, 229
Burmese mountain dogs, 228,
    231

Cairn terriers, 229
Canine bravery, medals for,
    20
Canine development, 29-33
Car-chasing dogs, 75
Car travel, 126-28
Carrying and retrieving, 187-
    90, 199-200
Castration, 237
Chesapeake Bay retrievers,
    199, 227
Chewing, 83-89
Chihuahuas, 229
Children, dogs and, 58-59, 69-
    70
Chows, 229
Chronic biters, 117, 233
Chronic chewers, 85-89
Circling, 31
Clipping, 34-36
Clockwork Orange, A (film),
    213
Cocaine, sniffiing out, 219
Cocker spaniels, 227
Collars, 140-41
Collies, 228, 231
"Come" command, 152-56
    heeling without leash and,
        167-68
Commands, brevity of, 68-69;
        see also Hand com-
        mands; and specific
        commands, for exam-
        ple: "Come" command;
        "No" command
Commercials, tricks for, 205-
    08
Communication, see Body
    communication; Words

Conditioning, 37

Consistency in training, 142-43

Correct position for heeling, 164

Cropping of ears, 232

Curly-coated retrievers, 199, 227

Curiosity of dogs, 121-22

Dachshunds, 228

Dalmatians, 229

Dandie Dinmont terriers, 229

Day, Laraine, 78

Death, 240-41

Defense pets, 215-18

Dental floss for use on dogs' teeth, 84

Digging, 33

Dingoes, 42

Discipline, love and, 27-28; *see also* Training

Distemper inoculations, 232

Diving, 200-01

Doberman pinschers, 228
  as attack dogs, 211, 219
  bite pressure of, 115
  as defense pets, 216

Dog pounds, 233

Dog runs in New York City, 124-25

Domesticated dogs
  dominance behavior of, 44-45
  pack behavior in, 43

Dominance behavior
  biting as, 52
  of male dogs, 43-46
  mounting as, 235

Downey, Robert, 46

Drinking, 77

Drugs, sniffing out, 219-23

Electric wires, dangers of chewing, 122

Electronic collars with microphones, to prevent barking, 110

English cocker spaniels, 227

English foxhounds, 228

English pointers, 227

English setters, 227

English springer spaniels, 199, 227

English toy spaniels, 229

Evolution of dogs, 29

Fear
  dogs, feared by children, 69-70
  dogs' reaction to, 55-56

Feeding, 76-82
  high-protein diets, 103
  as reward, 147
  vitamin deficiency, 86

Female dogs
  as attack dogs, 212-13
  giving birth, 238-39
  role of, 43, 46
  spaying, 237

"Fetch" command, 189, 191-94

Fights, 118-20
  breaking up, 119-20

Firmness in training, 143

Flat-coated retrievers, 199, 227

Fox terriers, 229

French bulldogs, 229

Funerals, dog, 240

Gadgets, dog, 23

Garfield, John, 20-21

Garland, Judy, 40

Gastric torsion, 78

German shepherds, 228
  bite of, 115
  breeding of, 231
  as defense pets, 216
  effects of jumping training on, 174
German shorthaired pointers, 227
German wirehaired pointers, 227
"Go" command, 184-86, 189
Golden retrievers, as water dogs, 199
Gordon setters, 227
Great Danes, 228
  breeding of, 230
  effects of jumping training on, 174, 178
Great Pyrenees, 178, 228
Greenberg, Dan, 42
Greyhounds, 228
  eyesight of, 37
  Italian, 229
  teeth of, 83
Growling, biting and, 107
Guard dogs, 216
"Guard this with your life" trick, 217

Hallucinogens, effects of, on dogs, 82
Hand commands
  associated with "sit" and "stay" commands, 144, 148
  in carrying and retrieving, 188, 190
  in "lie down" command, 159
  in trick learning, 173
Harriers, 228
Hashish, sniffing out, 219
Hatch-Metcalfe Law (New York City law), 236

Hearing, sense of, 40-41
Heated female dogs, 238
"Heel" command, 162-68
  leashes in, 164-68
Hepatitis inoculations, 232
Heroin, sniffing out, 219
High-pitched noises, aversion for, 40-41
High-protein diets, failures in h-breaking and, 103
Hip dysplasia, 231
"Hold it" and "drop it" command, 188, 197
Homosexuality, 235
Hoops, jumping through, 182
Hot-water bottles to calm crying puppies, 29
Hounds, sight and scent group, 228; *see also specific kinds of bounds; for example:* Bloodhounds; Greyhounds
Housebreaking
  basic, 90-96
  failures in, 102-06
  as imperative, 26
  mature dogs, 98-101
Human environment, adaptation to, 121-25
Human psychology, dogs irresponsive to, 24-26; *see also* Transference
Humans, dogs as, 22-24, 28, 61
Hunting, absence of sweat glands as evolutionary adaptation for, 33
Hurdles, 181

Identifying with one's dog, 23-25
Imprinting, 152
Inbreeding, 230-31

Inflated balloon tricks to stop dogs from jumping on people, 112

Inhumanity in attack dog training, 209-10

Injured dogs
biting by, 116
caring for, 31

Inoculations, 233

IQ tests for dogs, 25

Irish setters, 227

Irish spaniels, 199

Irish terriers, 229

Irish wolfhounds, 178, 228

Italian greyhounds, 229

Jackals, 29, 42

Japanese spaniels, 229

Jerking the leash in "heel" command training, 164-65

Jumping
learning, 173, 178-83
on people, 112-13

Keeshonds, 229

Kennel club registry, information from, 238

Kennels, 128-29

Kerry blue terriers, 229

Keys, use of, in "come" command, 153-54

Kill and maim, as function of attack dogs, 211

Killing habits, dealing with, 120

King Solomon's Ring (Lorenz), 54

Komondors, 228

Kuvasz dogs, 228

Labrador retrievers
black and yellow, 227

effects of jumping training on, 178
golden, 199, 227
as water dogs, 199

Lakeland terriers, 229

Leashes
dangers of, 123
getting used to, 140
used in "come" command, 152-53
used in "heel" command, 164-68
used in learning jumping tricks, 180-81
used in "lie down" command, 158

Left, learning to distinguish right from, 191

Legislation, 124
attack dog, 210
stray dog, 236

Leptospirosis inoculations, 232

Lhasa apsos, 229

Licking habit, 38

"Lie down" command, 157-61

Life expectancy of dogs, 30

Loeb Match Method, 97

Lorenz, Konrad, 54, 55

Love, training and, 39-40, 143

Love fallacy, 20-28

Love triangle syndrome, 56

Magazine size discrimination training, 14, 37, 192

Male dogs
as attack dogs, 211-12
dominance behavior of, 43-46
prime time of, 30

Maltese spaniels, 34, 229

Manchester terriers, 229

Man-dog association through-
   out history, 20
Marijuana
   effects of, on dogs, 82
   sniffing out, 219
Mastiffs, 178, 228
Mating, information on, 238-
   39
Mature dogs
   acquiring, 233-34
   housebreaking, 97-101
Mechanical watchdog devices,
   209
Mental development, rate of,
   30
Metal tinsels, dangers of, 122
Mexican hairless dogs, 34
Miniature pinschers, 229
Miniature schnauzers, 229
Mixed breeding, 236-37
Mounting, as dominance be-
   havior, 235
Movies, tricks for, 205-08
Muzzles, 110, 116

Newfoundlands, 228
   breeding of, 231
   effects of jumping training
      on, 178
   as water dogs, 199
"No" command
   in basic housebreaking, 94
   learning to use the word
      "no," 71
   in "sit" and "stay" com-
      mands, 145-46
Non sporting dogs, 229
Norwegian elkhounds, 228
Nuisance, dogs as, 27

Obedience training
   attack dogs lacking, 210
   learning tricks and, 171-72

sniffing out bombs and
   drugs and, 220
*See also specific obedience
   commands; for exam-
   ple:* "Come" command;
   "No" command
Obedience trials, 205, 229
Odor camouflaging, 39
Otterhounds, 199, 228
Our Puppy's Baby Book, 23
"Out" command, 184-86, 189
Overfeeding, 77-78
Owner-dog relationship, 14-28
   dogs' responses to masters'
      unspoken reactions, 54-
      55
   dogs taking advantages of
      masters' weaknesses, 60
   love in, 20-28
Owner training, 65-70
   basic, 137-41

Pack behavior, 41-53
   dominance in, 43-46; *see
      also* Dominance
   ritualized, 49-53
Pain, dogs' high tolerance for,
   32, 33
Paper training, 90-96, 105
Papillons, 229
Patience needed in training,
   139, 143
Pavlov, Ivan, 37
Pekingese, 229
Perfect dogs, mixed breeding
   to develop, 237
Perfumes, 35
Pet cemeteries, 240
Pet shops, 232
Philosophy of dog training,
   13-19
Physical development, rate of,
   30

Physical fitness, jumping and, 178

Picasso, Pablo, 240

Plant eating, 81

"Play dead" trick, 177

Pointers, 227

Pomeranians, 229

Poodles, 229
  clipping of, 34
  as water dogs, 199

Pound (Downey), 46

Praise
  in obedience training, 147, 153, 157, 158
  when to give, 110

Prime time of male dogs, 30

Pugs, 229

Pulis, 228

Puppies
  barking by, 108-09
  calming crying, 29-30
  effects of paper training on, 91-92
  nipping by, 114
  selecting, 227-32
  whining by, 107

Purebreds, breeding, 236-39

Rabies inoculations, 232

Rapid training for films and commercials, 206

Release words for "sit" and "stay" commands, 148

Repetition
  authority and, 137
  avoiding, in commands, 158

Reprimands, 71-75

Retrieving, 187-90, 199

Rewards
  being off the leash as, 168
  food as, 147

Rhodesian ridgebacks, 228

Right, learning to distinguish left from, 191

Ritualized pack behavior, 49-53

Rolling over
  as submissive act, 53
  as trick, 176, 177

Rottweilers, 228

Rural environment, effects of moving from urban to, 134

Russian wolfhounds, 22

St. Bernards, 228
  breeding of, 231
  effects of jumping training on, 178

Salukis, 228
  eyesight of, 37
  as oldest hunting dogs, 16*n*.
  as status dogs, 22

Samoyeds, 228

Scent discrimination, fetching by, 191-93

Scent-group hounds, 228

Schipperkes, 229

Schnauzers, 228

Scottish deerhounds, 228

Scottish terriers, 229

Sealyham terriers, 229

Seborrhea, how to determine presence of, 34-35

Sexual instinct, aggression and, 235

"Shake hands" trick, 172, 191

Shetland sheepdogs, 228

Shih Tzus, 229

Shock-collar training, 212-13

Shopping with dogs, 123, 124

Shopping tricks, learning, 195-96

Siberian huskies, 228

Sick dogs, caring for, 31

Side step, heeling in a, 167

Sight, sense of, 37-38, 41

Sight group hounds, 228

Silky terriers, 229

"Sit" and "stay" commands, 140, 144-51

breaking, 150

in carrying and retrieving, 187

in learning jumping tricks, 181

"lie down" command and, 158-59

"play dead" trick and, 177

praise given for responding to, 147

release words for, 148

three-part procedure involved in, 144-45

Skin

layer of fat beneath, as insulation, 33

loose-fitting, as defensive adaptation, 32

Skye terriers, 229

Sleep, when to put a dog to, 240

Sleeping arrangements, 61

Smell, sense of, 37-39

Sniffing out bombs and drugs, 219-23

Spaniels, 199, 227, 229

Spaying, 237

Sporting dogs, 227

Staffordshire terriers, 229

"Stand" command from a lying and sitting position, 160

Staring, implications of, 52-53

Status dogs, 22

Stein, Gertrude, 240

Stepping off curbs, keeping dogs from, 122

Straight line, heeling in a, 166, 167

Stray dogs, 235-36

Surfing, 201-03

Survival training taught by mothers at birth, 29

Sweat glands, absent from dogs' anatomy, 33

Tabasco sauce

coating electric wires with, 122

uses of, in housebreaking, 92-93

"Take it" command, 196, 197

Teeth, caring for, 84

Terriers, 229

Territoriality, 49-51

fights over, 120

Tervurens, 228

Thompson, Hunter S., 216

Ticking clocks to calm crying puppies, 30

Tones of voice, dogs reacting to, 55

Toy dogs, 229

Toy Manchester terriers, 229

Toy poodles, 229

Training

greatest form of, 173

as imperative, 25-26

philosophy of, 13-19

See also specific froms of training; for example: Housebreaking; Obedience training; Trick learning

Training leashes, *see* Leashes

Training lessons

duration of, geared to dogs' attention span, 139

duration of in "heel" command training, 166

Tranquilizers for air travel, 131

Transference, 59
    aggressive dogs and, 119-20
    ownership of attack dogs and, 210
    training and, 19

Traveling, 126-34
    by car, 126-28
    leaving dogs in kennels while, 128-29
    by plane, 130-31

Trick learning, 13-14, 171-75
    carrying and retrieving, 187-90, 199
    common sense and, 175
    fetching, 189, 191-93
    "guard this with your life," 217
    hand commands in, 172-73
    "hold it" and "drop it" command, 188, 195-96
    jumping, 173, 178-83
    for movies and commercials, 205-08
    "out" or "go" command and, 184-86, 189
    "play dead," 177
    rolling over, 176, 177
    "shake hands," 172, 191
    shopping tricks, 195-98
    time to start, 171
    water tricks, 199-205

Underfeeding, 78

Unpredictability of attack dogs, 211, 213

Urban environment, effects of moving from rural to, 134

Urination to establish territoriality, 49-51

Vitamin deficiency of chronic chewers, 86

Vizslas, 227

Walking the dog
    aging dogs, 240
    effects of not, 25
    with regularity, 99-100

Water dogs, 199

Water-retrieving, 199

Water tricks, 199-204

Weimaraners, 227

Welsh corgis, 228

Welsh springer spaniels, 199, 227

Welsh terriers, 229

West Highland terriers, 229

Whining, 107-08

White vinegar, uses of, in housebreaking, 92-94, 104

Whippets, 228

Wild dogs on Long Island shore, 42-43

Wirehaired pointed griffins, 227

Wolfhounds, 37

Wolfs
    evolution of, 29
    as pack animals, 42

Wooden dumbbells, uses of, 193

Words
    release, for "sit" and "stay" commands, 148
    understood by dogs, 55

Working dogs, 228

Yellow Pages, uses of, in stopping dogs from barking, 111

Yorkies, 34

Yorkshire terriers, 229